The Secrets of Police Aikido

Other Works by Bill Sosa

The Essence of Aikido (with Bryan Robbins) 1987

P.A.C.T. Manual (Police Aikido Controlling Tactics) 1993

The Secrets of Police Aikido

CONTROLLING TACTICS
USED BY LAW ENFORCEMENT
PROFESSIONALS

Bill Sosa

A Citadel Press Book
Published by Carol Publishing Group

Copyright © 1997 Bill Sosa
All rights reserved. No part of this book may be reproduced in any form, except by a newspaper or magazine reviewer who wishes to quote brief passages in connection with a review.

A Citadel Press Book
Published by Carol Publishing Group
Citadel Press is a registered trademark of Carol Communications, Inc.

Editorial, sales and distribution, rights and permissions inquiries should be addressed to Carol Publishing Group, 120 Enterprise Avenue, Secaucus, N.J. 07094

In Canada: Canadian Manda Group, One Atlantic Avenue, Suite 105, Toronto, Ontario M6K 3E7

Carol Publishing Group books may be purchased in bulk at special discounts for sales promotion, fund-raising, or educational purposes. Special editions can be created to specifications. For details, contact Special Sales Department, Carol Publishing Group, 120 Enterprise Avenue, Secaucus, N.J. 07094.

Manufactured in the United States of America

10 9 8 7 6 5 4 3 2 1

Library of Congress Cataloging-in-Publication Data

Sosa, Bill.
    The secrets of police aikido : controlling tactics used by law enforcement professionals / Bill Sosa.
      p. cm.
    "A Citadel Press book."
    Includes bibliographical references
    ISBN 0-8065-1932-0 (pb)
    1. Police patrol. 2. Arrest (Police methods) 3. Aikido. 4. Self-defense. I. Title.
HV8080.P2S59   1997
363.2'32—dc21   97-25649
                                                                              CIP

To police officers, security personnel, and all dedicated and serious students of Aikido

I humbly acknowledge my respect, gratitude, and love to the founder of Aikido, Morihei Ueshiba, for his unselfish dedication to universal peace. Through his legacy, I am able to share this light with those who are seeking truth on the path.

CONTENTS

Acknowledgments x
Foreword xi
Introduction xiii

1. History 1
2. Philosophy 6
3. Four Basic Principles to Unify Mind and Body 15
4. Shodo-o-Seisu 24
5. Physical Training 26
6. Aiki Taiso 35
7. Aikido Techniques for Restraining and Arresting 60
8. Awareness and Maintaining Self-Control 64
9. Police Officers' Testimony 102

Conclusion 109
Basic Aikido Terms 111
References 115

ACKNOWLEDGMENTS

I wish to express my appreciation and sincere thanks to the following people:

To my wife, Angela, for her help in editing the manuscript and for typing many paragraphs.

Lynn Fabia, for the countless hours spent typing and retyping. My thanks to her not only for her help and support in putting this book together, but for all the work she does in helping me with continuous projects in operating the Aikido schools.

Dave Fabia, a very talented Aikidoist and a good friend who does not know what the word no means when asked for help, and who took fall after fall while pictures were being taken.

Officer David Feucht, for writing the foreword and for doing such a great job of running the Grand Prairie school in my absence and for his assistance in the Fort Worth school.

Officer Rudi Panke, for all his help and support. A job is never too big or too small, and he is always ready at a moment's notice to provide a helping hand.

Andrew Grochowski, a tremendous help with his invaluable input, reliability, friendship, and spirit.

Brian Knopp, for his computer expertise. His talent was well used for this book. My thanks for his efficiency and willingness to work under pressure and for going with the flow of the changes.

Brian Earle, who generously offered his time and help. My thanks for helping me when I needed it most.

Oliver Martinez Jr., for his time and help.

Juan Rivera and Virginia Brandenberger for their help with the illustrations.

Also special thanks to all the others who contributed their hard work and positive energy to putting this book together.

FOREWORD

I have long been interested in martial arts. I was always impressed with the fancy high kicks, the knockout punches, and the blocks that broke boards or bent pipes. In the early 1980s I began my formal martial arts training. I learned the fancy kicks along with several different punches and blocks. I attended tournaments, getting trophies and injuries, but as I started to get a little older, I found my leg did not lift as high as it once did. Soon I became disenchanted and quit.

In 1987, I became a police officer. It was obvious that I would need more skills than were taught in the academy. As I gained police experience, several things became apparent. Sometimes the "opponent" is bigger, stronger, faster, and possesses advanced skills. You may also face more than one opponent at a time. Also, during this period of civil liability, a purely defensive block can be made to look extremely offensive.

After looking into several martial arts, I found Aikido in January 1989. Aikido's nonaggressive and noncompetitive nature makes it very adaptable to police-related situations. While studying Aikido, it became obvious that moving out of the way of a punch or a strike was preferable to trying to block it. It made more sense to quickly take a person down than stand toe to toe punching it out.

Like most people, I had doubts about myself and the art; however, I have been reminded of the effectiveness of Aikido several times. Once, I was called to an attempted suicide. A man had taken twenty-four Valiums and consumed a twelve-pack of beer. I could see him unconscious on the floor, and I had to make a forced entry into the apartment. When the ambulance personnel arrived, the man became violent and resisted treatment, but all I had to do was control the man's wrist. With all he had put into his body, I had doubts about whether a pin would work, but every time the man tried to move to get up, he would lie back in pain. On another occasion, a man weighing about two hundred and fifty pounds tried to tackle me. I dropped my center and then he was unable to move me. I dropped my weight further and the man found himself face down on the ground with me on top of him. A simple move allowed me to pin and handcuff the man.

Aikido has also helped to develop my sense of awareness. I control a situation by moving myself around to positions of advantage and readiness. Just as with the information you learned at your academy, in Aikido and self-defense you refine and improve what you have learned. Things that do not work effectively you do not use, while you practice and polish those you use frequently and with which you feel comfortable. I have found Aikido very effective and practical for law-enforcement purposes. It requires very little strength, and the techniques are effective without being brutal.

Since my start in Aikido, Mr. Sosa has been my sensei (teacher). I have found his teachings very informative and practical. His willingness to incorporate techniques that are not traditionally practiced in Aikido only enhances his teaching. His flexibility and constant updating and upgrading of the art help him keep up with the times. While tradition is important to Mr. Sosa, he believes practicality, combined with effectiveness, is of the utmost importance. If you follow and practice the techniques shown, you will not be disappointed in the least. Remember, your toughest competition will come from within.

I would like to thank Mr. Sosa for having confidence in me, not only in my writing ability, but as his student.

> David Feucht
> Burleson Police Department
> Burleson, Texas

INTRODUCTION

One of the goals of this book is to introduce the application of Aikido techniques to law enforcement officers' work. As in the case of any introductory text, it is very important to present the reader with some background information about the art. For that reason, the first chapters will cover the origins and philosophy of this beautiful art. It should be understood that the narrow scope of this book will limit my discussion of the origins and philosophy to a necessary minimum.

When I started my Aikido training I had doubts about the art's effectiveness, but I became a firm believer through the help of my wonderful teachers, and now am wholeheartedly devoted to the study of this art. After many years of training and interaction with my students, many of whom are police officers, I realized that most Aikido techniques are effective in arresting and restraining. Discussions with active police officers have led me to believe that there is a lack of comprehensive books covering such applications.

I will explain here how a traditional Aikido training program can be modified to suit today's law enforcement requirements. I believe that there is a strong parallel between the samurai of feudal Japan and today's law enforcement officers. Both were entrusted with maintaining social order. Of course, there are also fundamental differences, simply because today's social order differs significantly from that of feudal Japan. Obviously officers nowadays do not have absolute freedom to act as they please. The old saying "the goal justifies the means" cannot be applied anymore. In our changing social climate, it is also obvious that today's officers need to develop mental and physical skills that will allow them to cope with the dangerous situations they face at work without exerting excessive force on their subjects.

To prepare officers for their work, I stress the importance of maintaining a proper frame of mind during stressful or dangerous situations. The chapter dealing with the basic principles of Aikido provides a systematic way of achieving such peace of mind. It also provides a step-by-step approach to the cultivation of this calmness in even the most stressful circumstances.

From my early youth I have been interested in martial arts. In the beginning, I was taken by the physical aspects of martial arts training, and for that reason I undertook training in judo, karate, and boxing. But at that time I had already begun to wonder about the physical limitations of the human body. It was becoming apparent to me that physical strength alone had limited effectiveness and that there was a need for something more substantial. One day while talking to a fellow worker, I first heard of Aikido, which was just being introduced to the United States. That was also the first time I heard someone talk about the mental as well as the physical aspects of a martial art. Things that he had to say about Aikido really aroused my interest, and as soon as I could find an Aikido school, I decided to join it. That was the first step toward my beginning with this beautiful art.

Although already very inquisitive about subjects pertaining to the power of the mind, I approached my initial training in Aikido with some reservations. This art appeared very different from karate and boxing, which mainly relied on the physical strength of the student. But I was able to work through my initial doubts, and with time and patient direction from many good instructors, I began exploring all dimensions of awareness. Aikido classes inspired me to read many books on the mental aspects of human capabilities, and I continually researched self-help subjects and looked for their application in my martial art practice and in daily life. Slowly, my study in Aikido has turned into a lifelong commitment to this new art and to its propagation.

What is Aikido? The art of Aikido, as it is practiced today, is a fairly recent phenomenon. Nonetheless, it represents a firm link between the martial arts of the samurai era and contemporary practitioners striving to develop mind and body unification, with

Introduction

the hope of leading freer and more productive lives. Direct translation of the Japanese term *Aikido* into English discloses the profound differences between Aikido and other martial arts. *Ai* is translated as harmony, *Ki* as energy or spirit, and *Do* as the way. Therefore, Aikido can be loosely translated as "the way of harmonizing or blending with energy." This energy is not limited to any particular form. For example, it can be, an aggressor's energy, a friend's energy, or perhaps the energy of the Universe. In a self-defense situation it implies blending with an aggressor's energy—his strike or hold—and redirecting his intentions. In this way, the aggressor is neutralized; he is assisted to the ground into a controlled position. A joint lock or pin renders the aggressor harmless but causes him no permanent injury. The Aikido student does not take advantage of his control to injure, maim, or kill his opponent. He may use his skills instead to project the aggressor away from himself so that he no longer poses a threat.

Furthermore, the art's name alone indicates that the Aikidoist does not clash with his opponent. He does not directly block his opponent's strike, but rather blends with his opponent's strength and energy, to which we often refer as Ki (the concept of Ki will be covered in greater detail in later sections of this book). Besides being gentler, blending and redirecting an opponent's force is always more effective than physically clashing with it, especially when an opponent is physically bigger and stronger. An Aikido adept never assumes the role of an aggressor. What I am describing is a gentle, nonaggressive art of self-defense, an art that neither seeks to compete, nor win with brutal force, nor destroy others. In Aikido the goal is perfection of character and the unification of mind and body. There are also no contests or trophies as in other forms of martial arts. Our challenge is to continually develop our technique and spirit in comparison with ourselves rather than others. As stated by one of the prominent martial artists of the past—Musashi Miyamoto: "Today is a victory over yourself of yesterday; tomorrow is your victory over lesser man."

At the onset of any training, it is understood that it is beneficial to encourage students and show them the value of time spent on polishing their techniques. That is why, initially, Aikido students are motivated to train by advancing through the rank system (signified by belt color) and the status that this earns them in the dojo (pronounced "doe-joe," translated as the training hall). As time passes, the motivation for training changes. The ultimate goal is for the student to develop an understanding and internalization of the spiritual aspects of their practice. At that time the ranking becomes of secondary importance and is used to indicate those practitioners to whom beginners can turn for help.

In many ways, the spiritual side of Aikido is more complex and more powerful than the physical side. Although the two cannot be separated, the spiritual side quickly becomes the focus of the practice for many Aikidoists. The spiritual aspect will eventually find its way into the everyday life of all serious Aikido students.

Training in the Aikido arts is much deeper than simply learning throws and pins. As students progress and begin to understand and develop their techniques, they also begin to develop balance, grace, timing, and self-awareness. They realize that they have a responsibility to challenge themselves to gain a deeper level of study and understanding. When the physical Aikido arts are practiced with honesty and integrity, this same attitude should be allowed to permeate all activities of one's daily life. The students should also keep reminding themselves of the importance of applying the same principles in daily life, which in turn will increase the ability to interact with others in a more positive and productive way.

Once totally assimilated, the ideals of Aikido can be directly applied to any situation in which person-to-person interaction is required. One learns the meaning of harmonizing or blending, for example, in negotiating business transactions. Instead of clashing with the other side and attempting to destroy it, one learns to harmonize with its needs to attain a result that is mutually acceptable. Besides achieving the desired goals for all sides, this leads to a relationship that promotes trust and future negotiating success. Thus, the attitude of blending, taught in Aikido, helps strengthen relationships and improve interactions among everyone involved, in family relationships, in driving a car in traffic, and in relations in the workplace. The spiritual growth learned in Aikido can be universally compatible with all major religions and

Introduction

strengthens the doctrine of love and gentleness. Beginning students find themselves introduced to a new gentleness that can be more consistent with their daily religious beliefs and practices.

Aikido truly has a special meaning for each one of the hundreds of thousands of Aikidoists around the world today. For many it builds self-confidence and a more secure feeling in day-to-day living when facing potential physical attack or abuse. For some, the added security can eliminate bad thoughts or lead to a more positive and assertive existence. For others, it means throwing away an accumulation of anger, resentment, aggressiveness, and other negative baggage, enabling them to channel their energies in a more powerful and positive way. When we practice the techniques on the mat, the gentle art of Aikido puts us in spiritual and physical harmony with each other. When students pair off to train, their only task is to sincerely find their *Aiki*, the fundamental principle of blending with an attack.

Aikido's philosophy of "harmony and blending with energy," may be applied to daily life by anyone interested in self-improvement. Its main principles are the coordination of mind and body and taking advantage of every possibility to create peace and harmony. Aikido principles are based on the same principles of balance in the Universe. We are all part of the Universe, and its laws apply to all of us. When these laws are broken, disharmony and chaos enter our lives. As it will be often apparent later in this book, the scriptures remind us to know ourselves so that we may be truly free.

It takes time, diligent study, and devoted practice to get to know yourself, as well as to develop physically, mentally, and spiritually. With age should come wisdom, but this is not always the case, and if you look around, you will find this to be very evident. There are many confused individuals who choose to follow someone equally confused or misguided.

Learn to make time to really get to know yourself. Each individual has a purpose in life. For some, it takes time to find that purpose, but "seek and you shall find." Last, but not least, keep trying, and if you die trying, at the very least you went like a true warrior. If and when you give up trying, you have defeated yourself and your purpose in life. Again, if we may borrow from

Musashi Miyamoto: "Even if a man has no natural ability he can be a warrior by sticking assiduously to...the Way."

Let us not forget that Akido is, after all, a martial art, and abundant proof of its martial value exists today. As such it provides an efficient means of defending against one or numerous opponents. There are living eyewitnesses and documentary films showing the martial prowess of the founder of the art—Morihei Ueshiba. This is not limited, however, to the example of one extraordinary person. Time and again, demonstrations by his students and his student's students, have proven that pursuit of spiritual development does not lessen Aikido's validity as a martial art.

In recent years Aikido as a martial art has caught the attention of many people, including law enforcement personnel throughout the nation and worldwide. Since Aikido techniques are soft, subtle, and meant to control rather than to destroy an opponent, the takedowns, joint locks, and controlling methods can be very useful to law enforcement personnel. In most cases, pain can be a great motivating factor, and Aikido techniques can be extremely painful when one resists them. The level of pain is directly proportional to the level of resistance, so an opponent is controlled by using his own force against himself. Submission is just a matter of an attacker's ability to tolerate the pain.

Throughout the years I have had the opportunity of instructing many police and security officers. Most of those with whom I discussed arresting methods agree that many of the Aikido techniques are useful in their work. Many of these officers have already studied some form of martial art, usually a "hard" style that emphasizes bone breaking, kicks, and punches. Most of them also agree that with changing times, their arrest and control tactics need to be revised. Many officers have expressed an interest in having Aikido techniques available in written form meant especially for the use of law enforcers. Because of their urging, I decided to select several techniques based on the principles of Aikido. In this book, I offer effective arresting and controlling techniques that can be used in a police officer's line of work or for civilian self-defense.

Introduction

Aikido is a very diverse martial art with hundreds of techniques and variations. For this book, only a special few of the most simple and practical ones were selected. While the techniques are basic, they are nonetheless useful and can be practiced by all students. When executed in accordance with the basic principles of Aikido, these simple moves, blend beautifully with an opponent's energy without the need for advantage in size or physical strength.

At the risk of repetition, I think it is necessary to stress the noncompetitive nature of this particular martial art. I would also like to caution the reader that no book can replace a qualified instructor. These pages merely offer examples of how the art can be applied and should be used as reference material during readers' training under the watchful eye of their instructors.

The Secrets of
Police Aikido

1 History

Aikido is a Japanese martial art that was created in the mid-1920s. It evolved into its current form under the keen eye of Morihei Ueshiba (1883–1969), whose name can be translated from Japanese to mean "Abundant Peace." It is a most appropriate name for a man whose love and desire for universal peace greatly influenced the creation of this art. Through his engagement in the training of various martial styles, he assumed the role of a catalyst in melding different martial methods into a single system closely adhering to the principles of mind and body coordination. The drive and reasons behind his actions are best summarized by his own words:

> Even though our path is completely different from the warrior arts of the past, it is not necessary to abandon totally the old ways. Absorb venerable traditions into this Art by clothing them with fresh garments, and build on the classic styles to create better forms.

Although Aikido is relatively young in comparison to most other martial arts, its background is rich in culture and philosophy. It gained popularity after the Second World War, greatly due to O-Sensei's active participation in introducing the "art of love" to the West. It earned this nickname due to its promotion of "nonviolence," the philosophy of love and harmony comprised the basis of the beliefs of its founder. Of course, he understood the basic human need to defend oneself, but was totally against any form of attack on others. According to him an attack is proof that one is out of control. At the same time:

never run away from any kind of challenge, but do not try to suppress or control an opponent unnaturally. Let attackers come any way they like and then blend with them. Never chase after opponents. Redirect each attack and get firmly behind it.

He professed the same idea of "nonviolent" behavior outside of the dojo, and believed that there were no reasons for gender or racial differentiation in this or any art. Whoever was willing to live harmoniously with his or her environment deserved equal rights on the mat of the Aikido dojo. He hoped that the practice of these ideals would eventually spill into other aspects of our lives, creating harmonious and peacefully coexisting societies. This quote from one of O-Sensei's lectures probably expresses his philosophy and ideals best:

> The Way of a Warrior is based on humanity, love, and sincerity; the heart of martial valor is true bravery, wisdom, love, and friendship. Emphasis on the physical aspects of warriorship is futile, for the power of the body is always limited.

He deeply believed that through the practice and use of the principles of harmony (Aiki) one could purify his spirit and attain the greatest heights of human potential.

Morihei Ueshiba, internationally recognized as one of the finest martial artists, is often referred to as O-Sensei, which means "great teacher." In 1960, the Japanese government recognized his contribution to the spreading of education in arts, invention, and creative arts by awarding him the Medal of Honor with purple ribbon.

Ueshiba Sensei played a very active role in the promotion of his art beyond the borders of his homeland. Since Aikido's introduction to the Western world, there have been volumes of excellent publications on the subject. Many of them are translations of old cryptic instructional texts, but there are also numerous recent works by personal pupils of the founder of Aikido and their outstanding students that provide less esoteric explanations. One of the premiere representatives of the army of O-Sensei's students sent out of Japan to spread the knowledge of Aiki abroad is Koichi

History

Tohei. The discussion of O-Sensei's philosophy in the following paragraphs is based on the information presented in Mr. Tohei's book *What is Aikido?*, published in 1962.

Morihei Ueshiba, the only son of Yoroku and Yukio Ueshiba, was born in 1883 in the village of Tanabe in Wakayama Prefecture, Japan. As a youth, Morihei's physique was rather weak, and he preferred reading books to physical activities. The boy had a special interest in Chinese classics. Attempting to balance his son's interests, his father encouraged Morihei to take up sumo wrestling when he was about eight years old. From the beginning Morihei Ueshiba trained diligently. As his physical strength was improving he realized the importance of a strong body in addition to an educated mind.

Although fond of the books and reading and an excellent student of mathematics, Morihei could not find satisfaction in sitting in the classroom; he needed a more active way to funnel his energy. After only a year of middle school, his excitable personality drove him to leave the program and enroll in a *soroban* (abacus) academy. Before the year's end he was acting as a teacher's assistant. After completion of this program, he got his first job, as a tax assessor. Upon the enactment of an unfair new tax law directed at farmers and fishermen, he resigned his position to organize a protest.

With his father's blessing, Morihei then decided to try his fortune as a merchant. In 1901 he set out for Tokyo to start a small stationary supply store. When the store closed down after several months, he discovered a fondness for martial arts while studying Jujitsu (*Kito-ryu*) and swordsmanship (*Shinkage-ryu*). Eventually, a case of beriberi forced him to return home. Soon there was yet another change in Morihei's life: He married Itogawa Hatsu.

Around the turn of the century (1904) Japan found itself entering a turbulent relationship with Russia. Young Ueshiba enlisted in the army to take part in the Russo-Japanese war, which gave him an excellent opportunity to display his martial spirit. During this period he improved his strength still more and obtained his first instructor's certificate from Yagyu-ryu.

After the war he returned to Tanabe, but his adventurous spirit did not allow him to stay there for long. Morihei responded to a government call for volunteers to settle the wild land in Hokkaido, and persuaded more than eighty people to follow him. In the spring of 1912, along with his wife and two daughters, he began a dangerous trip to "the promised land." The hard work and austere life in Hokkaido helped Morihei to develop tremendous physical strength. Many wild stories came out of that period of his life, but one fact cannot be doubted: his meeting the legendary master of Daito-ryu Aiki-jutsu: Sokaku Takeda. This traveling martial artist introduced thirty-year-old Morihei to the invincible techniques of Daito-ryu Aiki-jutsu. By inviting Takeda to stay with him, and later by accompanying him on teaching tours, Morihei trained in this art extensively, but this infatuation with the personality of Sokaku Takeda ended with the message from Tanabe that his father was deathly sick.

After closing his business affairs in Hokkaido, Morihei immediately set out on the trip back home to see his dying father. During the trip he met and fell under the spell of one Deguchi Onisaburo, a "master" of a new religion called Omoto-kyo. Soon after his father's death, to the great dismay of the rest of the family, Morihei decided to undertake serious study of this religion, and by 1920 he was fully engaged in studies and Budo training at the head shrine of Omoto-kyo. He stayed with this sect for eight turbulent years, after which he was encouraged by Onisaburo to go out on his own and pursue his goals.

Morihei went to Tokyo, where he began teaching his art to a variety of students. The membership of Kobakan, his dojo, grew until the outbreak of the Second World War, when many students were lost to the war. In time Ueshiba grew tired of living in the big city and decided to move to the village of Iwama in Ibaragi Prefecture, which is now considered the birthplace of modern Aikido. Over ten years, beginning in 1942, he developed a systematic set of Aikido techniques and an underlying philosophy. After the war, O-Sensei took part in the creation of the Aiki Association (Aikikai) and the steady spread of popularity of Aikido. O-Sensei practiced his art until his death, on April 26, 1969. Since then, many of his great students have opened training centers in the United States. Two of them who provided the link to the original source of the "art of peace" are Koichi Tohei Sensei and Isao Takahashi Sensei.

Many practicing Aikido students of O-Sensei are known to enthusiasts of this art worldwide. Some of their names can be found in the bibliography at the end of this book.

2 Philosophy

Throughout his adult life, O-Sensei believed that the practice of Budo (a way of life through the application of martial arts principles) is the best way to create a better life and purify the heart. After difficult mental and physical training in many martial arts of Japan, he had mastered Hito-ryu, Jujitsu, and finally Daito-ryu. He had begun to question the real meaning of martial arts training and many aspects perplexed him. Was it not a waste of time and energy to train only the physical body? To be able to throw or hurt others and prevail over them, was that what martial arts were finally all about?

Master Ueshiba's intense desire for truth and knowledge led to the creation of Aikido. He urged his followers to focus on the cultivation of character through the combination of martial arts training and spiritual development. Being victorious over others had no attraction to the serious Aikidoist. He realized that today's winner will be tomorrow's loser, and that youth is usually accompanied by strength, which diminishes greatly with advanced age. While Aikido is a martial art that stresses self-defense, the emphasis in training is not so much on defeating an opponent as on defeating the enemy from within—our fears, egos, and insecurities.

It is difficult to formulate the crisp philosophical standing of the Founder and his art. Throughout his life he was a student of many religious trends and martial ways. From each he borrowed terms and phrases to help him explain his idea of peace and harmony. For that reason it is not surprising that many quotes of O-Sensei sound like Buddhist, Shinto, or Zen sayings. He pulled ideas from many different fields and dressed them in "new garments." Two major points evolved as main pillars of Aikido philosophy:

1. Cultivation of Ki.
2. Blending with Ki (Aiki).

The concept of Ki will be explained in detail in a later chapter. Suffice it to say now that it represents the primal energy borne out of the Void, the basic creative energy in life that transcends time and space. According to Kisshomaru Ueshiba in his book *The Spirit of Aikido*, "the principle of Ki was introduced into Japan in the Nara (710–94) and Heian (794–1185) periods, but the introduction of Buddhist thought from India via China affected its meaning, due to the idea of Karmic retribution." He continues, "the idea of Ki combined with indigenous views of nature, and it was taken to be the force responsible for the cyclical process of growth, budding, flowering and the withering of plants and trees.... The samurai who faced constant threats of death... understood Ki in terms of courage (Shi-Ki), willpower (I-Ki), vigor (Gen-Ki), and bravery (Yu-Ki)."

The second postulate of Aikido has to do with harmonizing and blending with Ki. It applies not only to physical training on the mat, but to everyday life situations. It is a way to develop a strong desire to live life without constant conflict and to bring about harmony through peaceful resolutions.

At first the concept of blending and harmonizing with an opponent's attack is difficult to understand. Even more difficult to comprehend is the idea that less is more. But blending properly with an attack leads to using the attacker's energy against himself to bring about an end result—and when this is done correctly the defender uses very little of his own strength: The more force the attacker exerts the less energy required by the one being attacked. It has been said by many that when the founder of Aikido threw them, they didn't know how he actually did it—but the one thing they knew for sure was that they had been thrown.

In his book *What is Aikido?*, Koichi Tohei writes, "At first I was skeptical and did not believe Ueshiba's arts were genuine." After attending a demonstration by the Founder, Tohei was invited to attack O-Sensei any time he wished. Mr. Tohei took off his coat and rushed with all his strength, and the next moment he found himself lying on the mat with no idea how he got there or what part of his body O-Sensei had touched. He thought that if he could understand what part of his body had received the power, he might devise a method of standing up to O-Sensei. As a Judo practitioner, he had enough confidence that he could throw any fourth-rank black belt student at the Keio University in Japan, but felt absolutely powerless against Ueshiba's art. Mr. Tohei was instantly impressed with Ueshiba and his martial art. He received permission to become Ueshiba's student, and went on to become one of the Founder's premier students, making the rank of tenth-degree black belt, highest in Aikido, and becoming a world renowned teacher himself.

Many years later, the author had a similar experience at the hands of Master Tohei. Mr. Tohei was teaching the principles of coordinating the mind and body and the proper use of Ki. He called me up front and asked me to bow from the seiza position. I knew how he was going to test me, but felt that since my center was almost touching the mat, I would be hard to move. It did not take long to find out how wrong I was. He knelt beside me and, using only his fingertips, pushed against my rib cage with such force that it sent me rolling onto my back, not once, but twice. The most interesting aspect was that I hardly felt anything where he touched me; instead I felt great energy on the opposite side of my body—almost as if I'd been shot out of a cannon. That one lesson was more than enough to convince me of the power of this magnificent art and what one can accomplish and develop through years of concentrated practice.

When properly learned, Aikido becomes a very powerful and effective method of self-defense that can neutralize any attack without causing serious injury to an aggressor, but numerous other benefits can be derived from training in Aikido. It helps to sharpen mental concentration, as the mind and body are trained to work together in a more efficient and harmonious way. This

Philosophy

type of training has no end and requires self-discipline, honesty, and concentration, with the ultimate goal for the Aikido student being the coordination of mind, body, and spirit.

The principles and philosophy of nonresistance are being studied and practiced by many Aikido students throughout the world. I sincerely believe that applying the blending aspects of Aikido can lead us to a better understanding of human nature and help us become better human beings. If more of us take the time to know one another, learn more about each other, and work together, we can achieve some measure of peace and harmony among our fellow men. We all have the capacity to make friends and not allow ourselves to be influenced by preconceived ideas or judgments. Keep in mind that we never really know who we are talking to when we first meet someone, yet it is highly possible that we can learn something from them. While first impressions are important, they seldom indicate the ultimate reality. In the business world, everyone we meet is a prospective customer or client, in politics or society a prospective supporter, and in life a prospective friend. Treat everyone with equal courtesy and respect, and do not let external appearances fool and mislead you.

In business relations prejudice can lead to unfavorable results as well. In 1955, at the age of twenty-one, I was excited about purchasing my first brand-new automobile. Over a long period of time, I had managed to save enough money for the down payment, and was about to make the most important purchase of my life. My excitement was quickly tempered when I arrived at the dealership. There were several salesmen milling around, but no one noticed me; they seemed more interested in amusing themselves with their jokes than making a sale. After I spent several minutes trying to get someone's attention, another salesman came out of his office and asked if he could help. I enthusiastically replied that I wanted to buy a car. He was very courteous and pleasant, and immediately we were able to work out the terms of a deal. Before we completed our business, he confided in me that he could not understand the attitude of the other salesmen. He said, "They only become enthused when an important-looking person walks in, and that attitude on their part is helping *me* become quite a successful salesperson."

Then he shared an interesting little story with me. One day a man walked into the showroom, which was located in an upscale part of northern Chicago. He was wearing work clothes, muddy shoes, and an old hat. The other salesmen ignored him, probably judging that he could not afford a new pair of shoes, much less a new car. When the salesman introduced himself and asked if he could help him, the man immediately replied, "I want to buy that car," pointing at the biggest, most expensive car in the showroom. The salesman said, "Fine," and asked how much of a down payment he was going to put on the car. "Oh, no," the man replied, "I'm paying for the whole thing right now." He then reached into his pocket, pulled out a large wad of money, and paid cash for the car.

These kinds of encounters can be witnessed almost daily. In any profession, you will find those who feel obligated to interact only with those who fit their favorable stereotypes. In Aikido, by working together on the mat, we are trying to discover these areas of our shortcomings. We learn that physical appearance does not necessarily convey proper information. Thus, the seemingly unrelated topic of self-defense can be extended to other areas of our lives. The only requirement on our part is that we listen carefully and give the training a chance to work.

While Aikido provides us with a positive vehicle for self-improvement and awareness, the dojo (the place where the Way is revealed) provides an environment for people from all walks of life to practice and learn together. It is meant to be a place for refining and developing the personality. This development begins by paying attention to such details as bowing before and after each series of techniques. Bowing shows respect for the other and allows us to clear our minds of prejudice prior to beginning the technique.

Some students are concerned about the religious significance of bowing. There is none whatsoever, it is only a gesture of acknowledgment and respect. In our Western culture, we shake hands when meeting someone, or say thank you when receiving a gift or favor. In the Japanese culture, all these functions can be fulfilled with a simple bow. Everyone has seen entertainers bow to the audience after a performance to demonstrate gratitude without

Philosophy

attaching any religious meaning to it. It is no different when we bow to each other on the mat.

In the propagation of peace efforts it is to our advantage to try to understand and respect other cultures. Like everything else worthy of our attention, in this art there are no shortcuts to proficiency. We must pay close attention to the details of the techniques and of etiquette on the mat. Self-discipline is part of the cultivation process, and self-discipline begins with regular class attendance. The real key to understanding and advancing is putting your body on the mat a minimum of twice a week, preferably three times. Know, also, that a teacher is only a guide trying to help you. The real responsibility lies with you, in taking advantage of the knowledge and learning to observe and practice correctly. There will be times when you will not feel like going to the dojo to train, and you are going to try very hard to convince yourself that there are "more important" things to do. (It is amazing how resourceful we can be in fabricating excuses when we do not feel like doing something.) At such times you should look at yourself honestly and take control of your mind. Doing so will automatically make you mentally and spiritually stronger. In Aikido, as in any training, there are no quantum leaps; progress arrives in very small steps. We need to appreciate every achievement, but at the same time we should not bask in its glory for too long. Through the years I have spoken to hundreds of students about this, and they all say basically the same thing: There were times when they did not feel like going to practice, but at the end they were glad they did, because they always came out refreshed.

Since Aikido is a very sophisticated martial art, it can often lead to frustration. This is especially true for beginning students. Remember that we all start with the same awkwardness and frustrations, but do not let this wear you down. Learn to cope with it by calming yourself and trying to determine its cause. Ask your training partner or your teacher for help in understanding the proper way to train and learn the techniques. Time and lots of practice are necessary in order to do the techniques properly. Learn to be patient with yourself. Your attacking training partner (*uke*) can be invaluable or a hindrance to your progress. In order to learn, there must be cooperation on both sides. If either uke or *nage* (defending partner) stiffens or uses too much resistance, this in itself becomes a form of competition that usually leads to a waste of time for both students. In Aikido training this type of behavior is called having a fighting mind. The cause is usually ignorance of the proper way of training and allowing the ego to control our actions. Remember that you are practicing to learn, and do not show off or fight with your partner.

One very important aspect of Aikido training is to develop a strong center, which is used in the execution of the techniques. Once a student develops his center and the ability to channel energy from it, his technique will become stronger, smoother, and easier to perform. He will use his entire body, rather than solely its upper portion. In order for the student to channel this energy into the technique, he must remain relaxed and in control of his body. The tensing of the body greatly impedes his flow of energy, and the tendency is to revert to using physical strength only. While physical strength is limited, blending and the avoidance of force are unlimited. Keep in mind, too, that everyone has so-called good days and bad days. There will be times when you will have a great practice session and your techniques work beautifully, and at other times nothing seems to work right. Do not be discouraged. Remind yourself that nothing works 100 percent of the time. Just as a baseball hitter does not make contact each time he steps into the batter's box, or a wide receiver in football doesn't score a touchdown every time he gets the ball, at times the Aikidoist will fail to execute a technique properly. When this happens do not despair, remind yourself that this is why the training is important. Always learn something from your failures, and find out how you can correct the problem in the future. The smart person learns from his mistakes and turns them into steppingstones for a deeper and better understanding of things. That is why we have this beautiful art today. Help make it even more beautiful by learning it well.

As humans, we are imperfect, and the Founder left us with the great gift of Aikido so we could polish ourselves and get closer to perfection. Look for ways to apply the magic of blending into everyday situations.

When we concentrate on small day-to-day crises, we lose sight of

Philosophy

what is important in our lives. Of course we need to deal with these issues when they come up, but if we don't keep them in proper perspective we will never get out of this "fire fighting" mode of operation. As Musashi Miyamoto suggests in his *Book of Five Rings*, it is important to see the distant things as if they were close and to take a distanced view of close things.

There are many different forms of martial arts. While they may differ in style and in the way they are practiced and applied, the underlying principles for all of them remain the same. The true foundation of all martial arts is respect, awareness, balance, timing, and the correct use of power. No matter how many different styles or techniques a student knows, without absorbing these fundamentals, the technical skills will be mediocre at best.

In my travels, teaching seminars in different parts of the country, I have the opportunity to meet and work with many different people who have black belts in several martial arts. Since they apparently haven't had the patience to study one art thoroughly, they often lack a sense of balance or knowledge of proper training concepts. Some students of martial arts study one art for a little while and then move on to a different one, barely skimming the top of each. I have nothing against crosstraining as long as a student stays in one art long enough to understand, in depth, the foundation and principles of that particular art. I believe it is best to excel at one thing rather than be mediocre in many things.

The study of martial arts in general, and Aikido in particular, is a way of life—with a long way ahead after reaching the rank of first-degree black belt. At this point it would be a grave mistake for a student to feel like an expert with nothing left to learn. When students come in and their first question is "How long will it take me to make my black belt?" they are only concerned with the symbol, and this detracts from the learning process and the true purpose of learning the art. The benefits of practicing Aikido derive from mental and emotional control, physical health, and spiritual awareness. The belt ranks are only symbols of a student's progress, and this progress is relative to an individual standard that is different for each student. Therefore people of the same rank will never be at the same level in all aspects of the art.

I am not trying to diminish the significance of earning a black belt, but it is important to stress the responsibility that comes with that rank. If a student has the drive to attain this rank, he or she must also show enough maturity to continue the refinement and internalization of his or her skills. It is worth repeating that it takes time and a lot of practice to get results from anything that is worthwhile. Patience is a mark of maturity and great virtue, and one has to learn patience while working toward a particular goal or level of proficiency.

Unfortunately, some people do not see the value of patience and are looking for an easier way. Consider a former student of mine who disappeared from his training for an extended period of time. Upon his return to the dojo, I asked what kept him away from our school. He replied that he had traveled to Jamaica to find his center. I asked whether his trip was successful, and he answered no. If this student and hundreds like him had learned to listen carefully to what I am saying, he would have known that his center was not to be found in Jamaica, or anywhere else he could travel to, for that matter. The center to which I refer is something everybody has to find *within* himself or herself.

Balance in life is important, whether applied to martial arts or everyday activities. In Aikido training, emotional and physical balance is of the utmost importance. In our training we are constantly aware of the center of gravity, which we believe is approximately two inches below the navel. It is often referred to as the one point or a point where the mind and body become integrated, resulting in the coordination of mind and body. When properly developed, this center becomes a point of balance.

3 Four Basic Principles to Unify Mind and Body

One of the ways Ueshiba Sensei actively promoted his art beyond the borders of his homeland was to send students abroad. One of the first and premier representatives of O-Sensei's students sent from Japan to spread the knowledge of Aikido was Koichi Tohei. He formulated the four major principles to unify the mind and body:

1. Keep one point.
2. Relax completely.
3. Keep weight underside.
4. Extend Ki.

These four basic principles can be found decorating the walls of many Aikido practice halls—but they are not mere decorations. These principles provide a constant reminder of their importance in the everyday training of Aikido adepts. In this chapter we will take a closer look at the ideas behind these basic principles.

You will recall that Aikido is a martial art emphasizing the development of physical and mental control over oneself and the situation in which one is placed. Therefore it should come as no surprise that the above principles refer to the physical (functional) aspect of the art as well as its mental (spiritual) side. Points two (relax completely) and three (keep weight underside) refer to the physical aspect of the art, whereas points one (keep one point) and four (extend Ki) govern its mental aspect.

Staying relaxed and balanced (keeping weight underside) is fairly simple to understand. The other two principles, namely keeping one point and extension of Ki, are more difficult to grasp. In addition, these two aspects are connected. Their interrelation constitutes the basis of the drive toward the mind-and-body coordination for which all Aikido students strive. This connection makes it impossible to adhere to one of the principles without total and unequivocal adherence to all of the others.

In gaining a fundamental understanding of Aikido, it is beneficial to analyze these principles using a "divide and conquer" approach. I will discuss each of these points separately, with support from the writings of such great martial artists as Musashi Miyamoto, members of the Yagyu family, and Morihei Ueshiba. Since Zen doctrine and martial spirit are closely related, and because of the very close ties of Soho Takuan —a Zen monk contemporary with these great samurai—with the Yagyu clan and Musashi Miyamoto, I will also offer his advice on mental bearing in combat.

The most obvious place to begin is with a discussion of the physical aspects of the art, which will be followed by a discussion of the more enigmatic psychological or spiritual aspect. Our analytical conclusion will attempt to put these pieces together, like pieces of a puzzle, to clarify the philosophical body of Aikido.

The easiest to observe, external characteristics of Aikido are its notably smooth, fluid, and circular movements, which result from an outstandingly well-balanced and stable position. In the words of Morihei Ueshiba:

> the body should be triangular, the mind circular. The triangle represents the generation of energy and is the most stable physical posture. The circle symbolizes serenity and perfection, the source of unlimited techniques. The square stands for solidity, the basis of applied control.

The use of geometric figures here helps to define the objectives of Aikido training. We must bear in mind that in previous statements *stable* and *balanced* do not refer to static conditions. Aikidoka are trained to maintain dynamic stability and continuous control while remaining nimble and extremely mobile.

KEEP ONE POINT

Beginning analysis of the mental aspect of this art with an idea of one point makes perfect sense. The environment in which we exist is enormous when compared to the size of the human body. In everyday situations, it is easy to perceive our body as the center of this environment, wherever we are located. This does not imply that we are the center of the Universe as we perceive it. It implies that from the standpoint of interactions between ourselves and our environment, we can locate the center of these interactions anywhere around us. It is helpful to mentally place it in the lower part of our abdomen. The state of continuous concentration of our mind upon this center is called keeping one point.

Many martial arts and religious practices center their teachings around the idea of maintaining concentration on the one point, although the location of the one point differs among the various disciplines. In Aikido, we must satisfy the seemingly contradictory requirements of being both stable and mobile, and the only way this condition can be mechanically satisfied is if the center of moving mass is placed in the lower part of the body and on the line of pivotal or turning motion. Such placement gives Aikido students a feeling of stability and allows them to move rapidly in any direction they wish. The center of any movement must be focused within the one point in the lower abdomen. By putting our attention onto the one point, we can preserve our stability no matter what happens.

Our one point must become a center for ourselves and for the actions around us. This way it also becomes the one point of the attacker, which he cannot help but follow. By the simple act of attack he has lost his own point of balance. Our one point has to take the guiding role in restoring that balance, and the only way to do it is to lead the attacker with our full control to a stable position on the mat.

In the book on swordsmanship, *Heiho Kadensho*, Munenori Yagyu states:

> If you release your mind, it will stay where it reaches. So, to prevent it from staying, we tell you to take it back, to bring it back, where it belongs. If you give a blow, your mind will

stay where the blow has struck. We tell you to find it and bring it back to yourself.

Bringing the mind *to yourself* refers here to bringing it to your one point and keeping constant control over yourself.

There is a fine line between concentration on one point and being "stuck" there. According to Soho Takuan, concentrating our mind in the area below the navel can be likened to trapping it there.

> If you consider putting your mind below your navel and not letting it wander, your mind will be taken by the mind that thinks of this plan. You will have no ability to move ahead and will be exceptionally un-free. When the person does not think of where to put it, the mind will extend throughout the entire body and move about to any place at all.

Takuan's major point is that putting too much emphasis on anything impedes progress in reaching an intended goal. He suggests that if we let our bodies naturally follow the principles, obtaining goals will be satisfied without our yearning to have them satisfied. This freedom, nonetheless, cannot be achieved without initially concentrating on the one point consciously, and the idea to which Takuan is referring comes from passing the conscious effort into our subconscious mind and letting it operate from there.

As a last remark to my discussion thus far, let me emphasize that keeping one point refers to the subconscious and instinctive process of maintaining our posture in such a way that the prior three principles are preserved at all times. This is the beginning of mind and body coordination.

RELAX COMPLETELY

A fundamental requirement, of which an Aiki student can never tire of hearing, is that of relaxing completely, often referred to as relaxing progressively. This slight distinction is made because of the unwelcome connotation associated with the state of being relaxed in a lifeless, or "collapsed," state. When an adept of Aikido is asked to relax, it is not a request to abandon vital alertness; nor is it a request to slump into a "drunken" state of idleness. To relax completely is to keep eyes open on activities around you. It is to maintain perfect awareness of everything and everyone present within your immediate vicinity. During practice in the dojo, it means being aware of the location of other participants in the class. Out on the street, it means being aware of what is happening at every single moment. As Musashi Miyamoto suggests:

> Both in fighting and in everyday life you should be determined though calm. Meet the situation without tenseness yet not recklessly, your spirit settled yet unbiased.

On the surface these may look like contradictory requirements, but they are not. To respond decisively and efficiently, to be able to assume a strategic position with an advantageous angle to an attacking force, requires complete relaxation and focus on your surroundings.

"Relax completely" is a seemingly easy, straightforward request, but those who have spent countless times on the mat trying to make this an instinctive and natural state are aware of the many pitfalls awaiting. Every one of us remembers how, at the beginning, it was so difficult to maintain a relaxed state of mind in the face of a partner readying for attack, real or perceived. In fact, with time we learned that perceived dangers pose a bigger hurdle in our effort to attain a state of relaxation, and that the practice of relaxation was closely tied to psychological conditioning. Initially, Aikido adepts have to work consciously on positive changes in their attitude. This stage is then followed by subconscious adjustments in their day-to-day personal outlook.

"Your attitude should be large or small according to the situation," directs Musashi, and O-Sensei adds, "A good stance and posture reflect a proper state of mind."

In addition to the obvious strategic advantage during a confrontation, staying relaxed has definite health benefits. Anxiety can lead to many health complications, among them the contraction of blood vessels, which in turn makes it difficult for the body to expel impurities. Without continuous "filtration," the human body is vulnerable and susceptible to countless diseases.

By practicing complete and progressive relaxation we are able to face each day with total control, rejuvenate our bodies, and remove the need to be nervous or excited in our daily life.

KEEP WEIGHT UNDERSIDE

In Aikido practice, just as important as the physical aspect of staying relaxed is the principle of keeping weight underside. The weight of physical objects is always naturally underside. Again, seemingly obvious observation creates many problems for beginning students. To *keep weight underside* means to maintain the stability of your "pyramid" without jeopardizing your mobility. Through years of social conditioning we acquire unnatural habits that prevent us from maintaining this otherwise instinctive state. Typical errors during the early stages of adaptation of this principle involve exaggerated stances that may appear "solid," but after closer scrutiny are obviously very vulnerable. For this reason, Aikido students are continuously urged to maintain the natural position during their training. Musashi Miyamoto offers this suggestion: "In all forms of strategy, it is necessary to maintain the combat stance in everyday life and to make your everyday stance your combat stance." Morihei Ueshiba makes this comment: "The key to good technique is to keep your hands, feet, and hips straight and centered. If you are centered, you can move freely. The physical center is your belly; if your mind is set there as well, you are assured of victory in any endeavor."

Keeping weight underside goes hand in hand with staying relaxed. When the body is aligned and relaxed, the force of gravity pulls every limb toward the earth along the supporting structure of the spine, hips, and legs. The importance of correct physical alignment of the body is evident in this detailed instruction offered by Musashi Miyamoto:

> With your features composed, keep the line of your nose straight with a feeling of slightly flaring your nostrils. Hold the line of the rear of the neck straight: instill vigor into your hairline, and in the same way from the shoulders down through your entire body. Lower both shoulders and, without the buttocks jutting out, put strength into your legs from

Four Basic Principles to Unify Mind and Body

the knees to the tips of your toes. Brace your abdomen so that you do not bend at the hips.

The moment alignment is disturbed, the force of gravity further exasperates the unbalanced state. Eventually this leads to the toppling of the entire structure. This is one of the basic premises behind the effectiveness of Aikido techniques. The person capable of maintaining balance while disturbing the balance of the attacker is clearly in an advantageous position. From this position, only minimal force is required to overcome an attacker. Aikido techniques apply momentum efficiently so that the attacker (nage) appears to be projected across the mat with minimal motion on the part of the defendant (uke). In this respect, Aikido is the art of accommodation of the attacker's initial intentions. One of the often-repeated O-Sensei's quotes is: "When an opponent comes forward, move in and greet him; if he wants to pull back, send him on his way."

Because of their underlying stability and centralization, Aikido techniques are swift, efficient, and powerful. At the same time this relaxed stable mobility makes them both beautiful and graceful. To the casual observer, nage appears to be drawing uke in and around to the final destination—the ground or a hold.

Now I can continue on to the next principle from Koichi Tohei's list, "Extend Ki."

EXTEND KI

A still more sublime aspect of the Aikido practice is the development of mind capabilities, which are indispensable during the later stages of body and mind integration.

Before I can analyze "extend Ki," I need to establish some basic ideas and terminology. Eastern philosophies perpetuate the belief that the possession of Ki (referred to as Chi in martial arts of Chinese origin) is not at all a sole privilege of human beings. This primordial energy flows through everything in the universe. Through social conditioning we often lose sight of the benefits of maintaining an alignment with Ki. Aikido training offers a systematic procedure to regain that contact. Through training we relearn how to utilize Ki in order to accomplish many tasks beneficial to us and our environment. We can use its circulation to purify our bodies as well as to energize and rejuvenate them. It can also be employed in helping us ward off opponents. As stated by O-Sensei, "Strength resides where one's Ki is concentrated and stable; confusion and maliciousness arise when Ki stagnates." In Aikido training the uninterrupted flow of Ki provides that stable source of power.

In any combative or confrontational situation it is important to maintain the positive attitude and extension of Ki. That is why Musashi tells us to instill vigor in our body. In simple terms, to extend Ki means to maintain a constant image of the flow of energy from the one point throughout our entire body. This flow is maintained through and beyond anything that happens to be in its path. The development of this feeling often is aided by the idea of "reaching into a distance." The mental activity behind this idea allows our body to remain calm, relaxed, yet unyielding and mobile. Yagyu's prescription for achieving this state is:

> With Ki always inside, a swift, effective response may come when needed.... If you maintain alertness in everything you do and accumulate experience, your Ki will become ripe.... If your Ki becomes ripe, it will extend throughout your body....

The tactical theory of Aikido is based upon the idea that emitted Ki creates a sphere of influence some distance beyond the center of our body. If we intercept an attacker at the right place on this sphere we will be able to take full control of his actions and incorporate them into ours under control of our one point.

As in any martial art, it is important to understand the basic principles that make it effective. It is also important to understand that these principles are meant to be applied all together at the same time. We cannot claim to adhere to one principle and be totally ignorant of others.

It is essential that the practice of Aikido, or any art for that matter, should be a long-term commitment. We must devote ourselves to the training long enough so that imitating our instructors can eventually become a creative process. Then we can devote ourselves to the true study of the art without being

Four Basic Principles to Unify Mind and Body

overloaded by its mechanics. According to O-Sensei: "In your training do not be in a hurry, for it takes a minimum of ten years to master the basics and advance to the first rung. Never think of yourself as an all-knowing, perfected master; you must continue to train daily with your friends and students and progress together in the art of peace."

One of the biggest challenges of Aikido training is to stay humble as you progress through the ranks. This sounds simple, but during practice students quickly find that doing so is very difficult and psychologically demanding. It is hard to accept a critical word from someone of lower rank, but if we remain aware of and work diligently at it, with time we can learn by listening carefully, and the mind and body begin to blend, coordinate, and relax, so that a peaceful mind and harmonious attitude develops.

As final advice, during training in Aikido techniques, listen to the instructions as if they were addressed to you personally and not to a group, because group psychology, sometimes diminishes the feeling of obligation to follow instructions. Never assume you know a particular exercise or subject; listen to each explanation and observe each demonstration as if it were being presented to you for the first time, and perhaps only time. At every level of development, there are always new elements to discover in each technique or instruction. How irresponsible would we be if we missed the sole chance to glimpse the "real thing" offered by our instructor.

Last, but not least, the instructor's critique is meant to open the students' eyes to the limitations they have placed on themselves through lifelong social conditioning and self-indulgence. Consider it a helping hand, not a slapping one.

4 Shodo-o-Seisu

Shodo-o-Seisu is another term that is difficult to explain fully. It means basically to control the first movement, both mentally and physically. The characteristic effectiveness of Aikido techniques comes from several factors. A physically fit body is a prerequisite for executing defensive actions. Awareness and sharp perception of our surroundings is also of great importance. But all this cannot come to life until we incorporate the principle of Shodo-o-Seisu in our training and daily life. Shodo-o-Seisu implies constant mental and physical readiness, and is especially relevant in the police officer's line of duty. This state of readiness is similar to that of an idling car engine, where all you have to do is press the accelerator to take off, rather than start the engine and wait for it to warm up. It is easy to see why the constant state of readiness is of great importance for police officers, who meet with the dangers posed by confrontation.

Ancient martial arts texts often state that a warrior cannot leave an opening for an attack. The warrior has to be in such a high state of awareness and physical fitness that it is impossible to catch him by surprise. The response to an attack must come without any hesitation. In his letters to the Yagyu clan, Soho Takuan states:

> There is such a thing as an interval into which not even a hair can be put. ... Interval is when two things come one upon another, and not even hairsbreadth can be slipped in between them. When you clap your hands and, just at that instant, let out a yell, the interval between clapping your

Shodo-o-Seisu

hands and letting out a yell will not allow the entrance of a hairsbreadth.

When practicing Shodo-o-Seisu, be prepared to welcome an attack, so that when it comes it appears that *you* are leading it. To be able to do that, you must be completely alert and calm, enabling you to use the principles of keeping one-point, staying relaxed, keeping weight underside, and extending your Ki. If the attack involves an initial grip on your wrist, have your arm ready by not letting your energy (Ki) stagnate. Allow it to flow freely, where you either break loose or turn it into a wrist or arm lock. Finally, these principles must be assimilated into, and allowed to govern, your daily life.

As the old saying goes, two wrongs don't make a right. If someone is angry and insults you, and you in turn insult that person a physical confrontation may result. If, on the other hand, you remain calm and in control of your emotions, it could be the first step toward a possible peaceful resolution. One of our Aikido students, a medical doctor who supervised several other doctors, shared this story with me recently: A couple brought in their five-year-old son for treatment for a throat infection. The parents wanted the doctor to inject the child with antibiotics, while the examining doctor wanted to take a throat culture first. The child resisted and locked his jaws to the extent that the doctor was unable to take the culture. At this point the parents, the doctor, and the nurse were all angry and frustrated. The situation was getting out of control, and the supervising doctor was called in. He calmly greeted the parents with a smile, asked what the problem was, and how he could help. The couple immediately calmed down and then were able to solve the problem to everyone's satisfaction. Remaining calm and open-minded is a method of controlling the first move so that good judgment can prevail. The doctor said that four years earlier, prior to his Aikido training, he would not have been able to handle the situation in such a positive way; he attributed his effectiveness to Shodo-o-Seisu.

5 Physical Training

If I say that most people are not in very good physical condition, no one can offer much in the way of an argument. Police officers are no exception. A police officer friend of mine twisted and broke an ankle while chasing a suspect through a parking lot. Another officer dislocated a shoulder trying to wrestle a suspect to the ground to handcuff him. A twenty-five-year-old Dallas police officer recently died of a heart attack after chasing a suspect for one hundred yards. Not too long before that, a twenty-nine-year-old officer died of a heart attack while trying to handcuff a man. When you read story after story in the newspapers about police officers dying at such an early age, it is not hard to conclude that many of them are not in very good physical condition. Physical fitness is of great importance, and a positive factor not only in doing better police work, but also in living a stronger and happier life. Please do not take it lightly.

Physical fitness should be important to everyone. When you are physically fit, life can be much more rewarding and satisfying. When you feel good about yourself, your attitude improves and you do an overall better job. Another good reason, probably the best one, to try to stay in shape is for your better health. One purpose in writing this chapter is to encourage police officers to get involved in a good physical conditioning program. Remember, you must get in shape and strive to stay that way. If you cannot make the time or do not want to get involved in a good martial arts school, where conditioning is part of the ongoing program,

Physical Training

then find a sport that appeals to you—one that is fun and at the same time rewarding. Here are some ideas: jogging, softball, swimming, bicycling, tennis, basketball, or volleyball. All of these can help condition the body, build strength, and improve flexibility, but whatever sport or program you choose, it is important to stick with it in order to get results. It is very easy to quit after just a few practice sessions. I have been asked whether I recommend weight training. My answer is always the same: I believe moderate weight training can be a plus for most individuals; however, strength with limited flexibility is not a very useful tool in most cases, and particularly in police work. At times law enforcement work can be very stressful, and a person who is physically fit will handle stress much better than one who is not. Faced with a confrontation, emotions usually intensify, the heart rate accelerates, and breathing becomes more difficult. Adherence to the precepts of Aikido and the required conditioning can be of benefit in lessening stress and insuring a positive outcome when confrontation does occur.

A very important phase of Aikido training is stretching, which is done at the beginning of each class. In the practice of any art, the healthy and supple body is as important as a flexible and educated mind. For that reason the discussion of the Aiki Taiso will be preceded by a presentation of the physical fitness and warm-up exercises. The benefits derived from stretching exercises are many. It is not only a great way to warm up the body before physical activity, it also helps in keeping the body flexible and toned, and is an aid to stability, balance, and maintaining stamina. Stretching will help relax and elongate the muscles and ligaments around the joints, allowing for a greater range of motion. This in turn helps improve circulation and efficiency, and lessens the risk of strain or injury. Most athletes are aware of this, and virtually all professional sports include some form of stretching in their training programs, recognizing the benefits of increased flexibility.

We can all learn a great deal by watching animals, particularly dogs and cats. These animals stretch their bodies often; it is second nature for them to stretch as soon as they get up from a nap. We can do the same when rising or even before getting out of bed in the morning. By taking a few minutes to stretch, you get the kinks out and energy begins to flow.

Try to get in the habit of stretching every day, even if it is only for a couple of minutes each time. If you cannot take the time to do all of the exercises outlined in this book, do a few each day. After you have been sitting at your desk or in your car for a while, get up and touch your toes a few times, making sure the knees are not bent. Then do back bends and reach for the sky, as in the Picking Fruit exercise. These are the first three exercises pictured in the book, and they can be done almost anywhere at any time.

The secret to success in anything is consistency. Continue doing your exercises until it becomes a habit. Soon you will begin to feel better and more energized. Although the exercises that follow are only a small part of our regular Aikido program, they are enough to help you stay flexible, as well as relieve stress and tension. For maximum benefit, perform each one with strong concentration for each part of the body on which you are working.

EXERCISES

TOUCHING TOES (FIVE REPETITIONS)

With legs straight, bend from the center, remaining loose and relaxed. The head should be dropped, and there should be no tension in the neck.

Physical Training

BACK BENDS (FIVE REPETITIONS)

Begin in a straight standing position, and with hands on hips, bend back from the center looking up.

PICKING FRUIT (MINIMUM OF TWO MINUTES)

Using visualization, stretch one arm, then the other over your head, as if picking fruit. Areas affected: all internal organs.

FORWARD STRETCH (MINIMUM OF TEN REPETITIONS)

With your legs together, stretch forward as far as possible. You should pull your toes back and keep the knees straight to get the maximum stretch. This stretch can be performed by holding the position shown or by sitting up and stretching forward. You should feel the stretch in your lower back and the backs of your legs.

SPREAD LEG STRETCH (MINIMUM OF FIVE REPETITIONS ON EACH SIDE)

To begin the stretch, spread the legs as wide as possible. Stretch the rib cage to the side, bringing the ear as close to the leg as possible, keeping the head between the top arm and leg.

Physical Training 31

BUTTERFLY STRETCH (MINIMUM OF TWO MINUTES)

Bring the soles of your feet together and pull your heels close to your body. Bounce your knees up and down in a rapid but gentle movement.

HIP STRETCH (TEN REPETITIONS)

Place both hands on your knees and gently push down.

MINI-SPLIT STRETCH (MINIMUM OF TWO MINUTES)

From the seiza position, spread your knees as wide as possible. Let the weight of your hips drop down and relax. You can also push your hips back toward your heels. Rock front to back to obtain a better stretch.

COBRA STRETCH (THREE REPETITIONS)

Place your hands under your shoulders and push up as high as you can comfortably go, leading with the chin. Keep the hips on the floor and arch the lower back. Come down slowly and relax completely for about ten seconds. Repeat.

Physical Training

LEG CROSSOVER STRETCH (THREE REPETITIONS ON EACH SIDE)

This exercise is intended to stretch the muscles of the hip and lower back. With your hands 90 degrees from your body (palms down), lift one leg up as high as possible. Roll the leg across your body and then look in the opposite direction. This exercise stretches and strengthens the lower back.

STOMACH CRUNCHES (MINIMUM OF THIRTY)

Knees should be bent and feet flat on the ground. Clasp your hands behind your head. Bring your shoulders and head forward. Try to put your chin on your navel. From the same starting position as the crunches, sit up and bring your right elbow to your left knee and your left elbow to your right knee.

KNEE ROTATION (MINIMUM OF TWENTY IN EACH DIRECTION)

With feet together, bend both knees and place hands above the kneecaps. Rotate in one direction, then the opposite direction. Focus is straight ahead. Areas affected: knees and nerves behind the knees. Helps to prevent arthritis.

6 Aiki Taiso

Each training session should begin with a good set of warm-up exercises. Once the student is fully warmed up and stretched, he or she should move onto the Aiki Taiso—commonly known as blending exercises. The order of the execution of these exercises is not really important. What is important is that they are understood and practiced correctly and with full concentration to help coordinate the mind and body.

The fundamental premises presented earlier come to life with the application of Aikido techniques for defense purposes. In order to be able to apply these techniques efficiently, aikido students must assimilate some essential body movements. To help in this process, a systematic method of practice will be illustrated. The number of different blending exercises is quite large, but only a few basic ones have been selected for inclusion here. The exercises can be practiced alone and can be done anywhere or anytime. They help develop posture balance, Ki flow, and proper body movement. I call them the Shadow Boxing of Aikido. The movements learned through the practice described in Aiki Taiso have direct application to the police arresting techniques presented later in this book. They should be practiced often, accurately, and with strong concentration.

During normal training progression, students begin by engaging in individual study. They are encouraged to work on proper postures, balance, awareness, and extension. Once the basic control over their own bodies is gained, students can then practice with a partner and add techniques to body movement. In the beginning of paired practice, students must concentrate on maintaining their composure in the presence of someone else. This has nothing to do with facing a conflict situation yet; it simply puts the students in more complex conditions. In this new situation students have to learn to bring harmony to their relationship with their partners, as prescribed by the basic principles of Aikido. This is the first step toward acquiring the ability to turn inner harmony outward.

For practical reasons, it is very important to stay close to the attacking person. Doing so allows you to "feel" the attacker's intentions and work within your range of power and control. You can continue to respond quickly by maintaining this close proximity. You also crowd his "zone of operation" by not allowing him to fully develop his strategy. In Aikido, this is called *ma-ai*, or proper body distance.

Finally, the role of correct breathing is of paramount importance in Aikido training and our daily life. Aikido students must cultivate deep, abdominal breathing in their training. Controlled abdominal breathing helps to release tension in the upper torso and utilize our lungs more fully.

People tend to breathe more shallowly as the circumstances around them become more intense or their physical output increases. This leads to less efficient use of the lungs and less oxygen in the bloodstream. As a result they tire more quickly.

Boxers use controlled abdominal breathing all the time. Seldom, if ever, do you see a professional fighter out of breath, even after many grueling rounds of fighting. They accomplish this by controlling the amount of air that goes in and out of their bodies. If you watch boxers train, you will probably hear a lot of grunting while they're punching the heavy bag. This grunting not only increases their power when hitting the bag, but also regulates the breathing process. Here are three very important points to keep in mind while you are training:

1. Do not hold your breath.
2. Keep your mouth closed.
3. Breathe normally when executing a technique.

Aiki Taiso

With time, as this process is integrated and becomes ingrained behavior, you will notice that you can ration your energy more efficiently during your training. After even more time you will notice that it is easier to stay calm during confrontational situations.

Breath control is very important in the early development of the Aikido student. It is also very important during his advanced training, but at that time the breathing process is already settled and the student can let it function on its own, without conscious effort. Musashi Miyamoto's suggestion "Do not let your spirit be influenced by your body, or your body be influenced by your spirit" reflects a higher level of development. Initially it is beneficial for students to encourage their spirits if their physical strength can support the effort, and for the spirit to entice the body for a little extra effort when the body needs enticement.

Once the student internalizes the basic principles of Aikido and polishes their application through a disciplined Aiki Taiso with correct, controlled breathing, the practical application of Aikido techniques, whether on the streets or on the mat, becomes instinctive and natural. Upon mastering these exercises, Aikido students are prepared to concentrate on the real problems during any conflict situation. Effectiveness is achieved because the mind and body work instinctively in harmonized unison.

Since students of Aikido spend a large part of their training throwing and being thrown, I'd next like to describe basic rolls, which will help you deal with your loss of balance during Aikido training.

KNEELING FORWARD ROLLS

Begin with the left knee up and your right leg tucked underneath you. Lower your body, extend your left arm just beyond your toes, and make sure your arm is on the inside of your leg. Your fingers should be pointed toward your body. Shift your weight to your front foot and slightly push off, keeping as much of your body as possible in contact with the mat. The roll should take you from one shoulder to the opposite side hip and not over the top of your head. Do not allow your arm to collapse. Your tumble should end in the original position from which you started. Repeat the same thing on the right side.

During these exercises it is very important that students concentrate on proper posture and unimpeded flow of Ki. It is possible—and important—to maintain good posture and total control over your body, even when you are falling.

As you become more familiar with forward rolls from the kneeling position, you can start performing the same exercise

FORWARD ROLL

Aiki Taiso

from a standing position. More advanced variations of this exercise involve a forward roll from a running start, leaping high and wide into the air.

The most advanced variation of this exercise involves one person leading (not throwing) the other down to the mat through a well-timed step in the original direction of the partner. Both the person leading and the person who ends up on the mat must remember all the prerequisites for correct Aikido technique during every moment of these exercises.

BACK ROLL

Start with your left knee up and your right leg tucked underneath you. The left arm should be parallel to the left side of your body, the right arm placed across your chest, touching your left shoulder. Sit down and look over your left shoulder. As you rock back, push off with the left leg to give you momentum and roll over the left shoulder. Straighten your right leg so that the ball of your foot touches the mat first. Shift your weight back to the right foot and keep your focus straight ahead. Keep your hands in contact with the mat to help maintain your balance. Allow your right leg to bend underneath you as your left knee rises up. You will end in the same position as you began.

Aikido practice often results in students falling down backward. This is an extremely uncomfortable situation for anyone to be in, but through the diligent practice of the back roll we can acquire the skill to allow us to recover from this position unharmed.

WRIST-STRETCHING EXERCISES

Many Aikido techniques rely on application of various locks and holds on attacker's hands. Some of these techniques derive their power and effectiveness from the fact that they inflict, albeit temporarily, pain in the joints of the arms to which they are applied. In order to comfortably participate in the reception of such techniques during practice, it is helpful to prestretch and warm up all joints.

BACK ROLL

Aiki Taiso

Kotegaeshi Undo (Reverse Wrist Stretching)

One of the signature defensive techniques of Aikido is called Kotegaeshi. It requires that a characteristic twist be applied to uke's wrist. The resulting pain from this pressure brings the attacker down to the mat. Kotegaeshi Undo is used to desensitize students to this temporary pain.

Begin by standing in a natural position. With your left palm facing you, fingers pointed upward, place your right palm behind your left hand and wrap the last three fingers at the base of your left thumb. Your right thumb should be placed between the last two knuckles. Stretch the hand by twisting to the left and lowering both hands to your center. Repeat this exercise several times on both sides.

KOTEGAESHI UNDO

Nikkyo Undo (Wrist Stretching)

The role of this exercise is to prepare the student for the reception of the defensive technique known as Nikkyo. This type of defense can be applied as a response to many different attacks.

Begin in a natural stance, then raise your left arm horizontally as if you were looking at your watch. The elbow should be slightly lowered and the shoulder down. Place your right palm over the left hand with emphasis over the first knuckle. As you simultaneously stretch the fingertips inward, the elbow moves forward for the proper stretch. Repeat several times on both sides.

NIKKYO UNDO

Sankyo Undo (Wrist Twisting)

This exercise prepares the student for the reception of the defensive technique known as Sankyo. This type of defense can be used as a response to various attacks.

Aiki Taiso

In a natural stance, look at the back of your left hand. The fingertips should be pointed downward. Wrap your right hand over the blade of your left hand, extending in an outward motion. Keep your elbow bent as you apply this cranking effect. Repeat several times on both sides.

SANKYO UNDO

Tekubi Shindo Undo (Wrist Shaking)

At the end of every wrist-stretching session, students need to allow the body to release the tension generated in the wrists. The Tekubi Shindo exercise provides this relief and dissipates the temporary discomfort that some of the wrist exercises must bring, especially in the early stages of practice. With time, students will learn how to apply just the right amount of tension, which will lead to the joints' expanded range of motion without causing undue discomfort.

Stand naturally with both arms relaxed and hanging down at your sides. Shake your wrists vigorously, then your arms, and then

TEKUBI SHINDO UNDO

your entire body from your center as you mentally allow tension to flow out of your body. Maintain a stable posture with all the members of your body fully relaxed throughout this exercise.

The next set of exercises allows students to develop concentration on their one point and the relaxation of their upper torso while executing many escaping techniques. Any holding attack requires that the uke drop his one point, and with relaxed upper torso begin the evasive movement of whatever defensive technique he chooses. During the execution of these exercises maintain the one point, breathe naturally, keep weight underside, and extend Ki.

TEKUBI KOSA UNDO

The purpose of this exercise is to teach students how to turn a wrist grab into numerous takedown techniques. Keep the flow of Ki uninterrupted throughout this exercise.

This is a low wrist-crossing exercise. Begin by starting with your feet about shoulder width apart and your hands at your

Aiki Taiso

sides. Start by turning both wrists inward and leading with the fingertips, crossing the wrists in front of your center. Return your hands to your sides and repeat.

TEKUBI KOSA UNDO

Tekubi Kosa Joho Undo

In this exercise the approach of the previous exercise is extended slightly. During the early stages of Aikido practice students have a tendency to raise their shoulders as they maneuver their arms around them. This is the result of the excessive use of upper torso strength. This exercise helps to overcome that approach and begin to use power generated from the one point.

This is a high wrist-crossing exercise, similar to Tekubi Kosa Undo, but in this exercise you will swing your arms up and cross your wrists at neck level. The purpose is to turn the wrist grab into a lead that puts you behind the attacker's arms. From this position a multitude of techniques can be executed to bring down an attacker.

TEKUBI KOSA JOHO UNDO

FUNAKOGI UNDO

The fundamental idea of uniting the entire body to accomplish a particular physical task is most evident in the exercise called Funakogi—a rowing exercise. It is named after its resemblance to the motion of the oar on the Japanese rowboat. In a most obvious way, this exercise depicts the application of weight underside, complete relaxation, and keeping one point during one continuous movement.

Begin in the natural posture with either foot forward. Before starting the exercise sink your weight onto your back foot with both of your shoulders relaxed and both of your wrists slightly curved and resting on the sides of your hips. It is very important to avoid raising your shoulders while trying to bring your wrists up along your hips. The weight of your entire body should sink down along the spine through your hips, which are squarely facing forward, through the center of the back foot. The forward foot should be lightly resting on the floor in front of you. This position should feel comfortable, with no strain exerted on any part of your body. Before starting the exercise students should

Aiki Taiso

consciously "check through" every section of their bodies for any undesired exertion or misalignment.

When satisfied that all basic positions are maintained, move the center of your body forward by shifting the weight from the back leg to the front one. As you settle your weight there, while maintaining the initial shoulders-spine-hips alignment, extend your wrists to full extension at the height of your hips. Then add to your motion the fourth element from the list of basic principles of Aikido—the extension of Ki. This is the unbendable arm in action. Make sure your arms are relaxed, and at the same time that Ki is flowing through them. Maintain the gentle, downward curvature of the wrist and allow Ki to flow uninterruptedly from the one point through the straight upper torso, along slightly curving arms out into infinity.

Next comes the return to original position. As in all Aikido techniques, this portion of the exercise begins with the hips (the location of the one point). Shift your weight to your back leg and allow this action to propel your wrists into a motion that will bring them back to their original position along the sides of your hips. The alignment of the upper body should not be affected by this motion; the shoulders and the hips must remain in alignment and squarely facing forward.

FUNAKOGI UNDO

Although it might seem trivial at this moment, maintaining total awareness of the entire body will become very important as soon as you begin the practice of this exercise with a partner. The partner's role is to provide you with incremental resistance, which will, at every stage of the exercise, challenge your ability to adhere to the principles of Aikido. The only way to retain stability in a relaxed manner is to single-mindedly apply yourself to proper execution of the exercise. When going forward, your body and your mind have to go forward, together. When pulling back, your mind and body must also act in total agreement.

Paying attention to details at this stage will make a world of difference when facing a real opponent. You will be able to stay relaxed and judge the situation with a clear, unclouded mind. It will also allow you to concentrate on the actions of your opponent without losing sight of other activities around you. Your senses will be sharpened so that you will be able to make any adjustments to your initial response in accordance with a developing situation.

SHOMEN UCHI IKKYO UNDO

This exercise is an application of the basic principles of Aikido and the idea of "direct entering" in order to efficiently respond to a direct attack. Shomen Uchi refers to a blow to your head, and Ikkyo means "first technique." As one of O-Sensei's students, Mitsugi Saotome explains in his book *The Principles of Aikido* that the basic principle of Ikkyo is to take control of your enemy's spirit. The essence of Ikkyo lies in taking control of an encounter from the first moment. You must enter and take over your enemy's spirit with the fearlessness embodied by the principle of Irimi.

Irimi constitutes a very important idea that is prevalent in all serious martial arts. This idea of single instantaneous response is very closely related to that of instinctive reply found in a single cut in Japanese swordsmanship.

As in Funakogi Undo, begin in the natural posture with either foot forward. Before starting the exercise sink your weight onto your back foot with both of your shoulders relaxed and your arms hanging down. Again, as in the Funakogi Undo, the weight of

Aiki Taiso

your entire body sinks down along the spine through your hips, which are squarely facing forward, through the center of the back foot. The forward foot should rest lightly on the floor in front of you.

Imagining a blow to your head (*Shomen Uchi*), move your one point forward by shifting your weight from the back leg to the front one. This motion will generate force, which in turn will propel your arms forward and upward. The arms will come to rest with hands above eye level, elbows slightly bent, and Ki flowing freely upward and well beyond your physical reach. Of utmost importance here is not to translate extension into overextension outside of the base of balance formed by your triangularly positioned feet. Later, during actual application, when there is a need for additional distance to be covered you will accomplish that by taking a follow-up step. This sliding step will allow you to cover the required distance without jeopardizing your balance.

Next, shift your weight to your back leg and allow this action to bring your outstretched arms back to a relaxed position along your torso. Do not allow the flow of Ki to waiver through your arms at any time during this exercise. If someone were to push up on your arms while in their natural position at the sides of your torso, they should remain relaxed and unbendable.

SHOMENUCHI IKKYO UNDO

Throughout this exercise, and previous ones, your intention should be directed forward whether you are moving forward or backward. Even while pulling back we should not retreat in a cowardly way; we are simply assuming a new strategic position, with full awareness of the environment and situation around us.

ZENGO UNDO (TWO-DIRECTION EXERCISE)

This exercise brings additional complexity to the one previously described—a pivot around the vertical axis of your body. Thus, it is a two-direction exercise using exactly the same movement as Shomen Uchi Ikkyo Undo. Its purpose is to teach students how to close a gap and extend awareness to 100 percent as they turn in both directions.

Begin by sliding forward with the left foot, followed by the rear foot as you swing your arms upward, leading from the fingertips. When lowering your arms, make a slight fist with your hands and drop your arms to your sides. Turn 180 degrees to your right, sliding forward with the right foot followed by the rear foot again, swinging your arms forward and up. Drop your arms to your sides, pivot to your left, and repeat the exercise several times.

ZENGO UNDO

Aiki Taiso

HAPPO UNDO (EIGHT-DIRECTION EXERCISE)

An even more advanced version of Shomen Uchi Ikkyo Undo is called Happo Undo. This exercise teaches students how to maintain both awareness of their surroundings and the basic principles of Aikido while turning and pivoting in eight different directions. The purpose is to extend the mind 100 percent while turning in each direction, covering 360 degrees.

For the sake of simplification, imagine that you will be facing the four walls, and then the four corners, of a symmetrical room.

1. Slide forward with the left foot followed by the rear foot, then turn 180 degrees to your right.
2. Slide forward with the right foot followed by the rear foot, then turn 90 degrees to your left.
3. Slide forward with the left foot followed by the rear foot, then turn 180 degrees to your right.
4. Slide forward with the right foot followed by the rear foot, then turn 45 degrees to your left.

HAPPO UNDO, STEPS 1 TO 4

5. Slide forward with the left foot followed by the rear foot, then turn 180 degrees to your right.
6. Slide forward with the right foot followed by the rear foot, then turn 90 degrees to your left.
7. Slide forward with your left foot followed by the rear foot, then turn 180 degrees to your right.
8. Slide forward with the right foot followed by the rear foot, then turn to your left. You will now be facing the front again. Repeat the exercise several times.

HAPPO UNDO, STEPS 5 TO 8

TENKAN UNDO

It is often required to allow a direct attack to run its course while moving out of the way in search of the appropriate response. The Tenkan—wrist-lead—exercise provides a way to develop this ability. Using this approach you will provide a stable point which will

Aiki Taiso

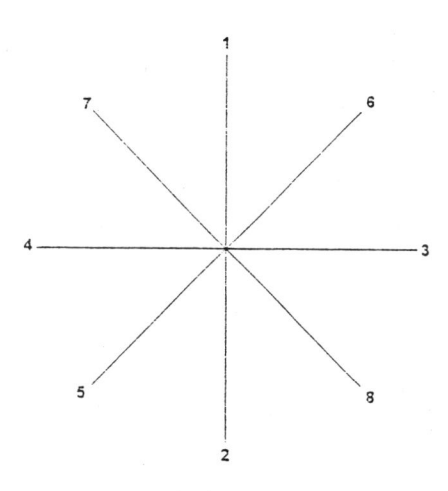

```
        1
  7  \  |  / 6
       \ | /
  4 ----+---- 3
       / | \
  5  /   |   \ 8
        |
        2
```

DIAGRAM OF HAPPO UNDO (EIGHT-DIRECTIONAL EXERCISE)

become a center of motion of both bodies—yours and your attackers. As in Funakogi Undo, you will begin the training as a solo exercise and move on to practice with partners.

As in previous exercises, begin in the natural position with either foot forward. Spread your weight between your front leg and back leg. Extend one of your arms forward with your wrist gently bent and your fingertips pointing toward your *hara* (one point). Your arm represents yet another form of unbendable arm, with Ki freely flowing out of your center through your upper torso and along your outstretched arm into a distant target. Check that all parts of your body are aligned and relaxed.

Next imagine someone grabbing your wrist (later have your partner actually do it). If you started with the same arm forward as the forward foot, without changing the condition of the arm in front, slide forward with the front foot and pivot on it. If you started with the opposite arm, take a step forward with the back foot and then pivot on it. Bring your back leg behind in a circular motion, providing momentum for the entire movement. The wrist of the extended arm provides the pivoting center for this entire action. Throughout this movement keep your back straight, keep the Ki flowing through your arm and out of your bent wrist, breathe in a deep and controlled manner, and maintain awareness of your environment. Repeat the exercise, alternating sides.

When practicing with a partner, remember the basic principles of Aikido while maintaining proper distance from your partner. One difficulty in this more advanced practice is that the resistance provided by your partner creates distractions that make it difficult to keep control over your own body. Although this may sound contradictory, make sure you do not try to control your partner. Keep in mind that if you have control over yourself, you will eventually be able to control your partner or opponent.

TENKAN UNDO

Aiki Taiso

SAYU UNDO

As I have stressed, all Aikido techniques require a solid, balanced posture and the ability to maintain the unbendable arm and weight-underside principle. This exercise teaches you how to accomplish both.

Start in a natural posture with your arms hanging relaxed at your sides. Your feet should be lined up about shoulder width apart and your focus straight ahead. Swing both arms to your left with the left arm comfortably extended and your right arm to your center. Both palms should be turned upward. Keeping your back straight, lower your center by bending the left leg slightly and

SAYU UNDO

straightening the right leg. Next, swing your arms to your right as you return to the straight position, and repeat the exercise on your right side.

The more advanced version of this exercise requires you to swing your arms, make a shoulder-width step to the side, and then settle into a balanced position.

UDEFURI UNDO

In this exercise the motion of your hands begins with a slight movement of your hips. The body has to be in full alignment with its vertical axis—you should not wobble.

UDEFURI UNDO

Aiki Taiso

Begin by placing your feet about shoulder width apart and your arms on the right side of your body. Swing your arms to the left and right, much like the motion of windshield wipers. Your body should remain in a very stable, unmoving posture while your arms swing from side to side. Mentally allow all tension to flow out of your body while doing this exercise.

UDEFURI CHOYAKU UNDO

Besides providing the means for the body to relax, this exercise shows you how to align your body in motion with its pivoting axis. Normally this exercise is performed right after Udefuri. As you end Udefuri with the count of "three, four," take a step forward with your left foot, slightly pointing your left shoulder forward and down. The left hand is at your one point while the right hand is at the small of your back.

Begin by shifting your weight forward by sliding your left foot forward, take a step with your right foot, pivot, and step back with your left foot, turning 180 degrees. Finish by drawing the right foot back, the arms swinging freely in the direction the body is turning. The left hand will be in the small of the back and the right hand settled at your one point. Repeat the exercise moving forward with the right foot and continuing the same movement.

UDEFURI CHOYAKU UNDO

KOKYU DOSA, "THE GRANDFATHER OF ALL AIKIDO EXERCISES"

Since all Aikido arts employ the principle of Kokyu Dosa, this great exercise not only has to be understood, but highly developed as well. The effectiveness of all the technical aspects of Aikido has to do with proper understanding and application of the Kokyu Dosa principle. This exercise teaches the development of a strong center (one point) and the importance of strong Ki flow—as well as the proper connection with uke, which has to do with the points of contact, in this case uke's grip on nage's wrists. These points of contact and nage's center must become one, enabling nage to disrupt uke's balance for easy control and takedown. The four basic principles of mind and body coordination discussed earlier are extremely important in performing this exercise correctly.

Kokyu Dosa is done in the kneeling position (*seiza*), giving more emphasis to moving from the center without the use of the legs. To start this exercise, uke also kneels, facing nage, and nage comfortably extends his or her arms, elbows down and slightly bent. The hands should be open and the fingertips should be pointed slightly upward. With uke firmly holding nage's wrist, nage starts his or her movement, from the center. Moving the center straight and forward also moves the arms and wrists forward, with the entire body behind it. It is very difficult for uke to maintain his or her posture, since hand power by itself is no match in stopping nage's body movement. As soon as nage's balance is disrupted, nage leads uke onto his or her back. At this point, nage quickly moves his or her body next to uke's and continues to extend energy downward, holding uke to the mat. This is a wonderful exercise that teaches both nage and uke how to give and receive energy for proper training in Aikido.

Aiki Taiso

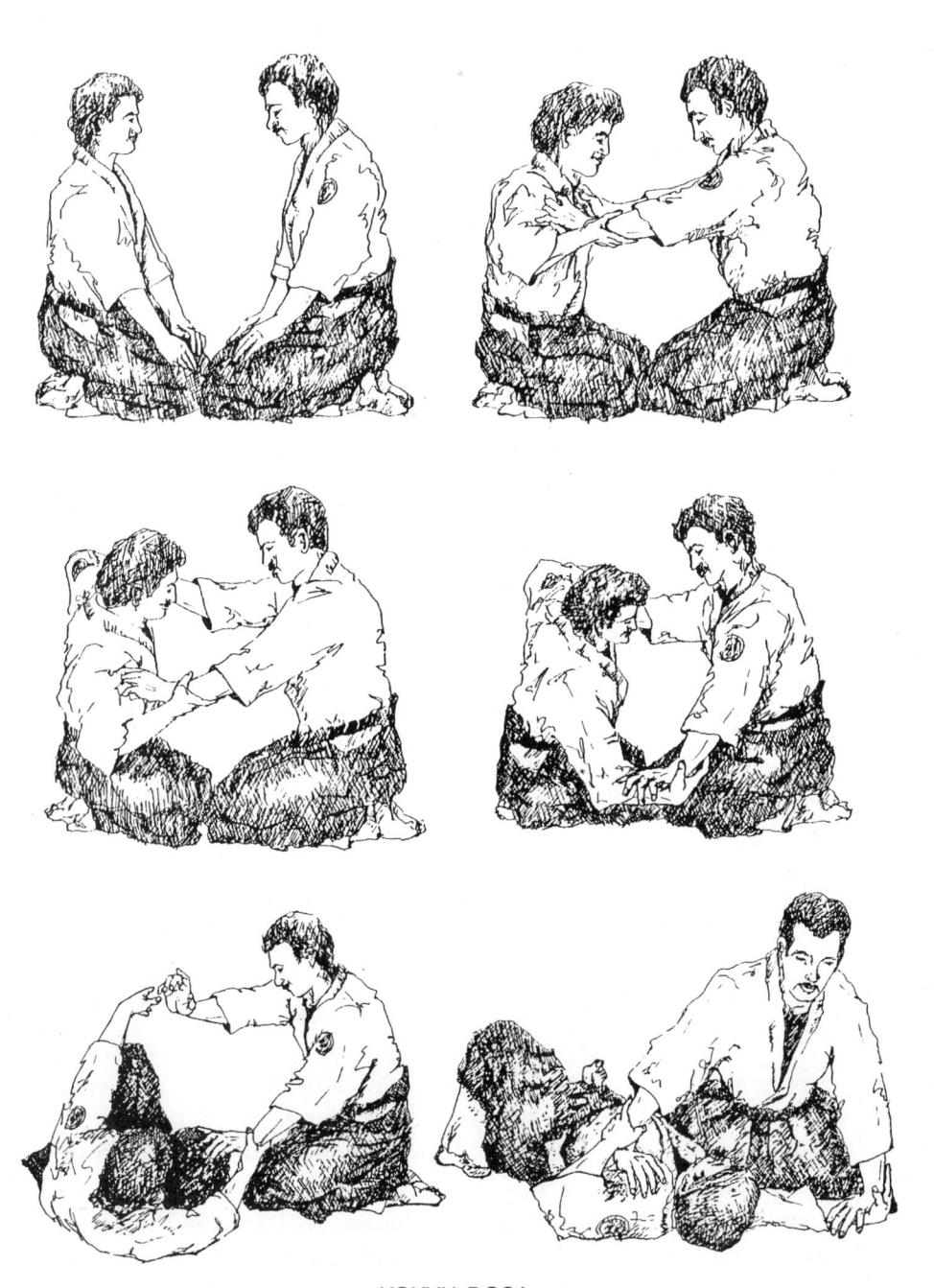

KOKYU DOSA

7 Aikido Techniques for Restraining and Arresting

So far I have discussed the physical preparation of the body and spiritual bearing of the mind during Aikido practice. I also pointed out, more than once, the fact that Aikido techniques provide a very efficient means of self-defense. The very same techniques can be effectively used for arresting and restraining a subject in a controlled manner. Aikido controlling and self-defense techniques do not require great strength in order to be effective.

"Controlled manner" is of special interest to the law enforcement community, in part because of the recent surge in lawsuits against police departments throughout the nation. More and more police officers and departments are being sued for alleged police brutality or for using unreasonable and excessive force, with resultant suspensions or terminations of the officers involved. If law enforcement officers are taught and encouraged to use proper tactics and reasonable force in arresting situations, we may very well see a decline in lawsuits filed against police departments. Before I began to write this book, I talked with many police officers to see what I could learn from them that would help me with the project. Their major complaint was basically the same, no matter what city or state they came from. After graduation from the police academy, they felt that they were not getting adequate training on arrest and control tactics. Many of the officers also expressed concern that the training they had received in the academy was insufficient and outdated, or even that it was taught in a way that encouraged the use of excessive force. Many martial arts are currently taught, and they all have something good and positive to offer. Many martial arts offered in police department curricula are taught as competitive sports with the objective to down an opponent with force, but the liability factor may arise when force is met with force. Only enough force needed to bring a situation under control should be used.

A police officer is in a position of authority, with which comes the responsibility to be self-disciplined and to make sound judgments. In an arrest the police officer must safely control the suspect and deliver him or her to the proper institution. The officer's safety should always be of primary concern, but whether we like it or not, a suspect's safety is also important. A suspect resisting arrest does not necessarily present an opportunity for nightstick practice. If officers do not exercise self-control, situations may sometimes become very nasty. One only has to recall the Rodney King case in Los Angeles or the Malice Green case in Detroit. Cases like these can be the beginning of the end of a police officer's career, in addition to causing very costly damage to the department.

Searching a suspect is one piece of police work that can often develop into a very dangerous situation for the arresting officer. Suspects who find themselves being searched often feel violated, humiliated, and embarrassed, particularly when others are standing by watching, and according to statistics this is when a subject is most liable to turn on a police officer. To help minimize a violent reaction from a suspect, it is important to handle this part of police work tactfully and cautiously. An officer often has no way of knowing whether he is dealing with a mentally disturbed person, someone under the influence of drugs or alcohol, someone with a hidden weapon, or a combination of these things. The suspect should be kept as calm as possible by talking to him or her and explaining what is about to happen, how long it will take, and that cooperation will expedite the process. There are a great number of searching techniques used by various police departments, each of which has its own benefits. This portion on search is not meant to be a manual—more a reminder to do a thorough job. A careless body whisk does not constitute a good search. Whatever methods of search you are now using, whether you start from the waist and work your way down and then up, or start at the top and work your way down, make sure you conduct a complete search. A good search must be thorough, complete, and systematic. If you are doing a systematic search of the upper body first, you may start with the waistline. Feel the entire waistline area, checking the back thoroughly as well as all front pockets. The inside of a hat and even the hair on some people can conceal a weapon. The cuffs on pants, shoes, and boots are an ideal place to easily hide knives, razors, and guns. Remember that knives, guns, and many other types of weapons can be strapped to just about any part of the body: arms, legs, or ankles.

An Aikido student of mine who is a police officer told a story about being searched by another officer after being stopped for a traffic violation. The officer being searched was in street clothes and didn't tell the other officer that he was searching a cop. He was spread-eagled against his car and searched, but the searcher overlooked the gun strapped to his ankle. A mistake like that could be fatal. An alert cop would not make such an error, knowing it could cost his life. Regardless of the sequence you use, it is less likely that you will forget or overlook some area if your search is performed systematically.

Below is a set of rules to keep in mind when approaching a suspect and performing a search. During any confrontational situation, physical or not, when your adrenaline is pumping, it is best to stay calm and aware of your surroundings. It is of great benefit to have a systematic set of points, such as the one that follows, to rely on:

RULES TO KEEP IN MIND WHEN APPROACHING A SUSPECT

1. Where are the suspect's hands?
   - (a) in his pockets
   - (b) behind his back
   - (c) Is he holding something?

Aikido Techniques for Restraining and Arresting

2. What is available that the suspect could use as a weapon against you?
   (a) rocks
   (b) bricks
   (c) sticks
   (d) beer bottles or other objects within reach

3. Who is with the suspect who might interfere with the arrest and possibly come to his aid?
   (a) friends
   (b) relatives
   (c) sympathizers or bystanders

4. Routes of escape
   (a) Where are they?

5. What kind of terrain are you standing on?
   (a) slippery or uneven surfaces
   (b) gravel or rocky area
   (c) icy, wet, or muddy
   (d) curb
   (e) crowded area

This systematic approach coupled with an awareness of anyone and anything in the vicinity will help you through many difficult situations.

8 Awareness and Maintaining Self-Control

Awareness is the number-one requirement in any self-defense situation. If you are not aware of an oncoming attack, you will not be able to defend yourself against it. Controlling the first move is extremely important, and in order to respond properly you must stay alert and calm. In fact, it is always desirable to be calm and in control. The only certainty in life is uncertainty. No one knows for sure from one minute to the next what may happen. Police officers' methods of defense can vary drastically from one situation to the next. They may be required to jump and take cover behind an automobile if someone is shooting at them, or struggle to retain control of their weapons. Awareness means not only being aware of a suspect's physical and emotional state, but also your own. In order to control the first move, you may first learn to control yourself. In Aikido we call this "keeping one point," or in plain English, staying centered and calm, in control of all your physical, emotional, and spiritual faculties. Doing so in adverse conditions is not easy for most people, but with sincere practice it can be achieved, as it must be in order to make better assessments and keep a situation under control.

When approaching a suspect, it is important to be aware, courteous, and respectful, to approach him or her in a defensive rather than offensive way. By using this approach, you are already applying the very basic and fundamental principles of self-defense. Remember, every action brings about a reaction. If you

Awareness and Maintaining Self-Control

approach someone in an offensive manner or posture, it could very well trigger his opposing reflex. Even thieves and thugs like to be acknowledged in a positive way. Always use a professional and polite approach. The word *please* is really a magic word that should be used more frequently by all, including law enforcement personnel.

Many people do not like the power and authority associated with law enforcement officers. I have come across numerous people who are against the establishment and dislike authority of any kind. They feel threatened by it and build strong resentment toward all police officers and view them as their enemy. I heard a story from a police officer who had been in a very nasty struggle with a man who attempted to kill him with a gun. After the man was subdued, arrested, and calmed down, the police officer asked, "Why were you trying to kill me? I do not know you nor have I done anything to you." The man replied, "It had nothing to do with you personally. I don't even dislike you. It's that uniform you are wearing. I have been talked down to, shoved and pushed around, and mistreated by cops in the past. Every time I see a police uniform, it just sets me off." By being professional and proper, you could be helping fellow officers who may run into this person in the future.

An officer must learn to develop his perceptions to acquire immediate and fundamental knowledge through the use of his senses. In Aikido practice, we develop our intuition, or the so-called sixth sense. I remind my students that they must learn to see and hear with their entire bodies, not just their eyes and ears. Being able to quickly see through a situation gives you the upper hand to deal with it before it gets out of control.

This book has many practical techniques, but technique is not the whole story. Techniques alone will not be enough to stand up to the apathy, insults, and danger that police officers inevitably face. In fact, technique alone will let you down when you need it most, unless it is coupled with something else. People call this "something else" by many different names. It includes such attitudes as courage and commitment, but that is not all. I think of it as "inner strength" or "spiritual strength," meaning that your inner self has been so developed that you approach each situation you face with a sense of balance and connection to a power greater than yourself. Some get this inner strength from a strong belief in God and their religious faith, some from family tradition and the way they were brought up. Others derive it from strong commitment and dedication to their job.

A dedicated martial artist develops himself through the study and practice of his art. In keeping with tradition, many people study martial arts for inner development and well-being as much as for self-defense purposes. The samurai is the role model for many martial arts students and could be a model for a police officer as well. Like the samurai, you have been given a position of power in society, since you are called to dangerous situations where you must act quickly and with a kind of courage the average citizen does not have to exercise. To do this you need to train in technique as a samurai trained. He mastered technique, in his case, swordsmanship. In time of crisis, technique came to him so naturally that he was able to execute swiftly and spontaneously. He was able to do it without thinking; however, the samurai also saw the need for inner development so that he could apply his technique swiftly, skillfully, and calmly, even in the face of death. Part of this came from knowing what he truly believed in—the warrior's code of ethics. The other part came from following spiritual practices, such as meditation, to calm his mind. Like him, you also need to develop your inner strength by doing the same two things.

First, just like the samurai, you need convictions—your own code of values. You can attain this by developing a strong sense of what you believe in and what you are committed to accomplishing. This comes from reflecting on what you have been taught about your duty and by developing your own personal philosophy of what you think it means to be a police officer. You may want to reflect on your training and discuss ideas with others. Read and learn all you can. Your convictions have to be so well thought out that you know what you believe in, regardless of the pressures of any situation. The second thing you should do is develop an inner calm, like that of the samurai. You should remain so calm inwardly (keeping one point) that your own mind does not churn with thoughts and emotions that prevent you from

Awareness and Maintaining Self-Control

carrying out your duty. There are many paths to developing this inner calmness, such as learning to detach yourself from a situation, calling on your religious faith, or following a practice such as meditation. The end result should be that no matter what feelings you have inside—discouragement, anger, fear—you proceed and do your job. Inner calmness allows you to control your mind and your body so that your emotions cannot deter you from using proper tactics. In this state of mind, your techniques will flow out of you to handle any situation in which you find yourself.

Lastly: Do not take your work home with you. Balance is the key between your role as a police officer and your personal life. It is admirable to strive to be the very best that you can be at all times, regardless of your line of work, but you cannot be a cop twenty-four hours a day without draining yourself physically and emotionally. A strained relationship with family and friends often results from becoming obsessed with your job. To many, police work is a very satisfying career. It is just a career, however, not a way of life. When your shift ends, put the day's events behind you. Learn to relax, let go, and enjoy your life.

Following are some Aikido techniques that can be used by police officers and Aikido practitioners in other walks of life. All should be used with caution, preferably in conjunction with supervision in a program offered at your dojo.

TECHNIQUE NO. 1

The opponent grabs the defender's weapon with his right hand from behind. The defender grabs the opponent's hand with his right hand and turns in a circular motion, raising the opponent's arm. With his left hand on the opponent's elbow, the defender continues in a circular motion. The left hand then goes under and over the opponent's arm, removing the weapon and throwing the opponent down.

Awareness and Maintaining Self-Control

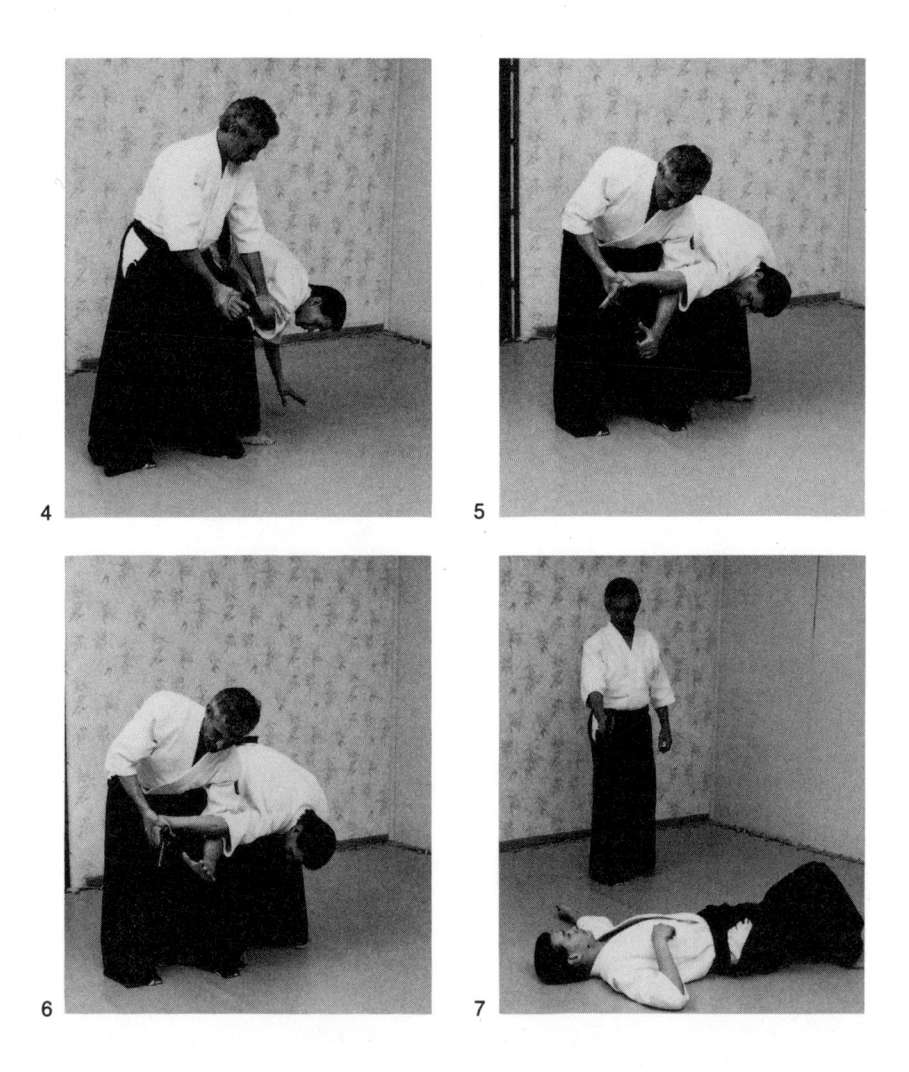

69

4

5

6

7

TECHNIQUE NO. 2

As the defender begins to draw his gun, he is grabbed from behind by the wrist and choked. The defender lowers his chin and steps back with his left foot as he draws his gun. He applies *Sankyo* (wristlock), takes the opponent down, applying a controlling pin, and removes the weapon.

Awareness and Maintaining Self-Control

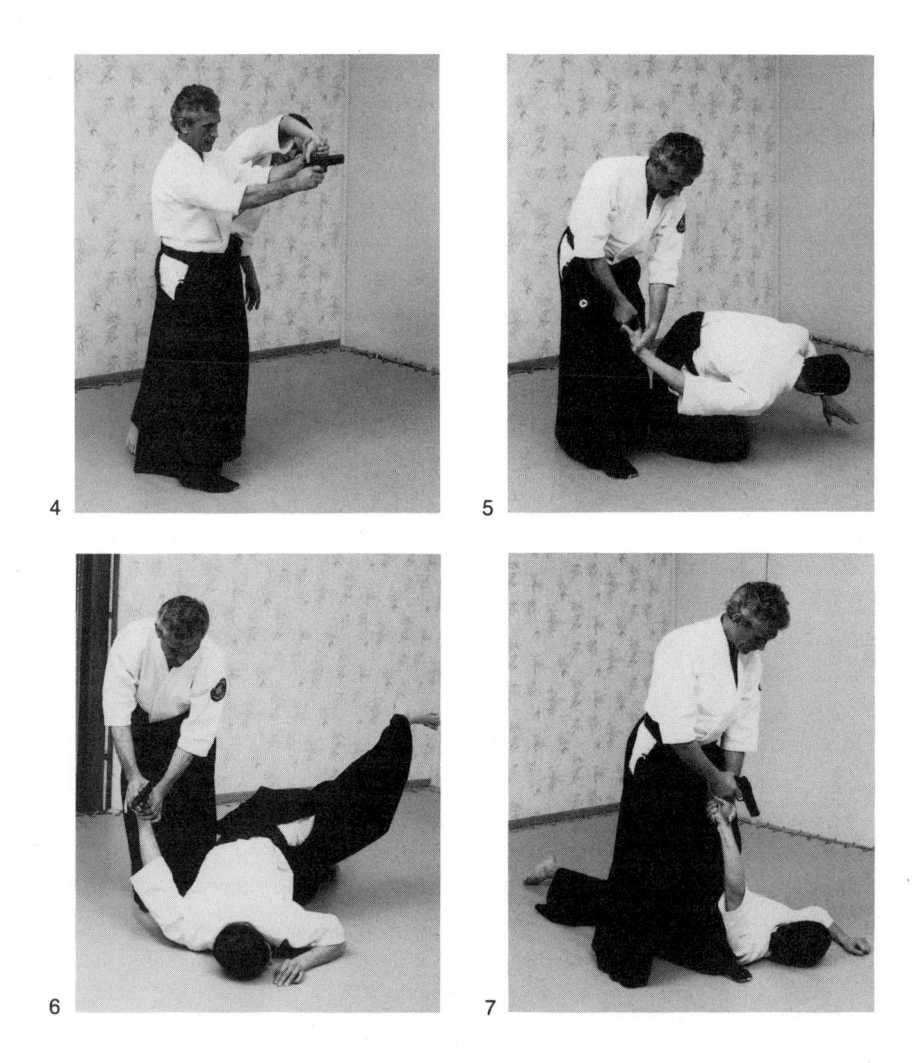

71

4

5

6

7

TECHNIQUE NO. 3

As the defender begins to draw his gun, he is grabbed from behind by the wrist and choked. The defender drops his chin, pulls down on the choking arm with his left hand, then turns to his left and leads the opponent down with his right hand.

Awareness and Maintaining Self-Control

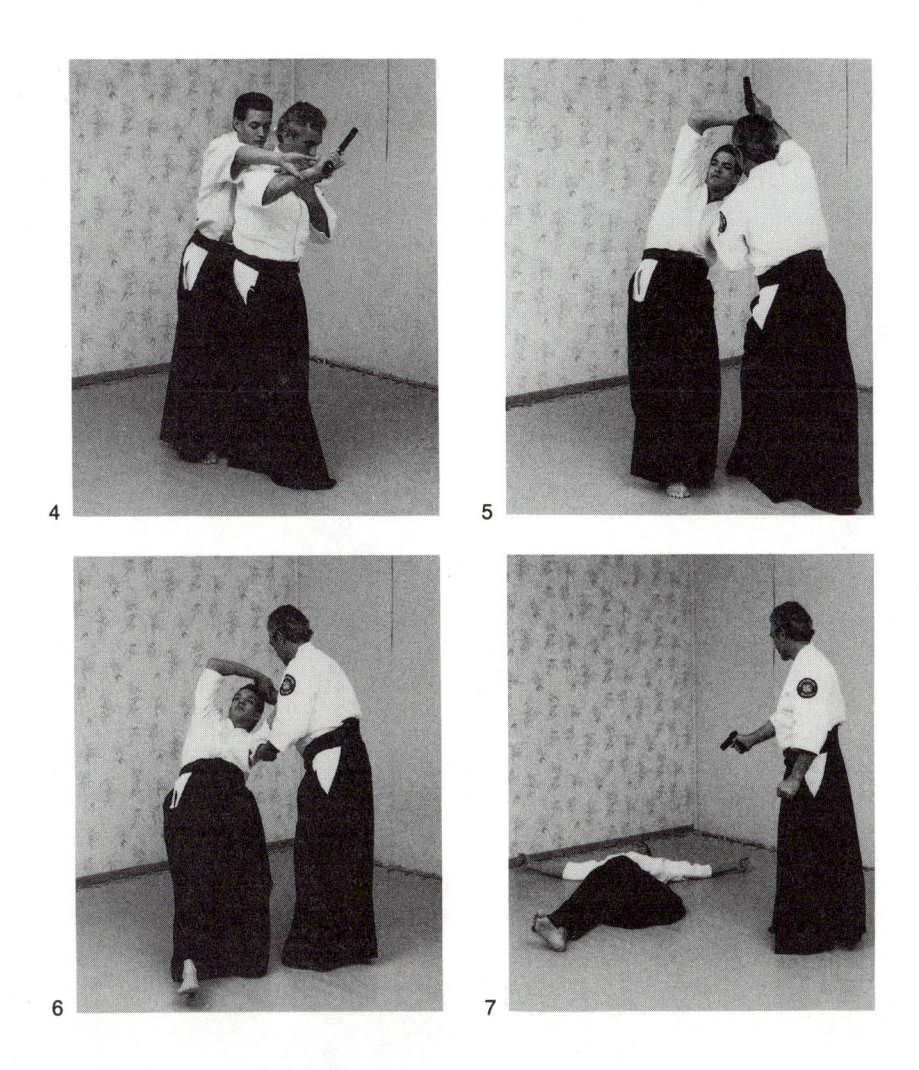

4

5

6

7

The Secrets of Police Aikido

TECHNIQUE NO. 4

The defender has the gun in his hand and is grabbed by both wrists from behind. The defender raises his right hand as he steps back in a position to control the elbow, snakes his left hand around the opponent's right arm, and brings him down with a controlling pin.

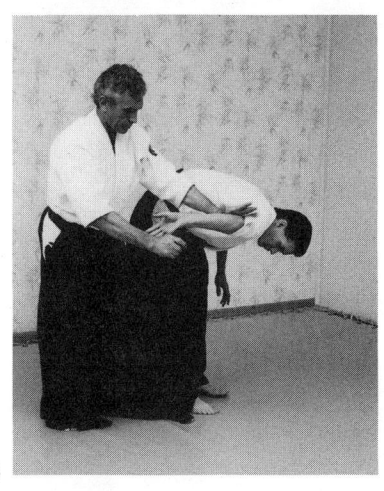

Awareness and Maintaining Self-Control

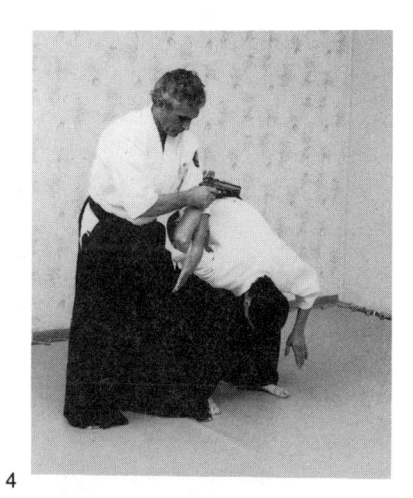

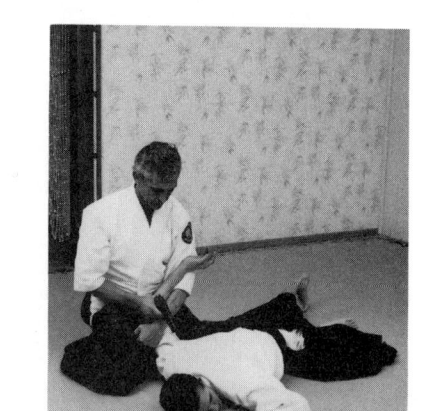

4

5

TECHNIQUE NO. 5

As the defender attempts to draw his gun, the opponent grabs the defender's right wrist with both hands from behind. The defender draws his gun by lowering his center and turns to his right, placing his left hand around the opponent's neck, and in a semicircular motion leads the opponent to the ground, and finishes with a controlling pin.

Awareness and Maintaining Self-Control 77

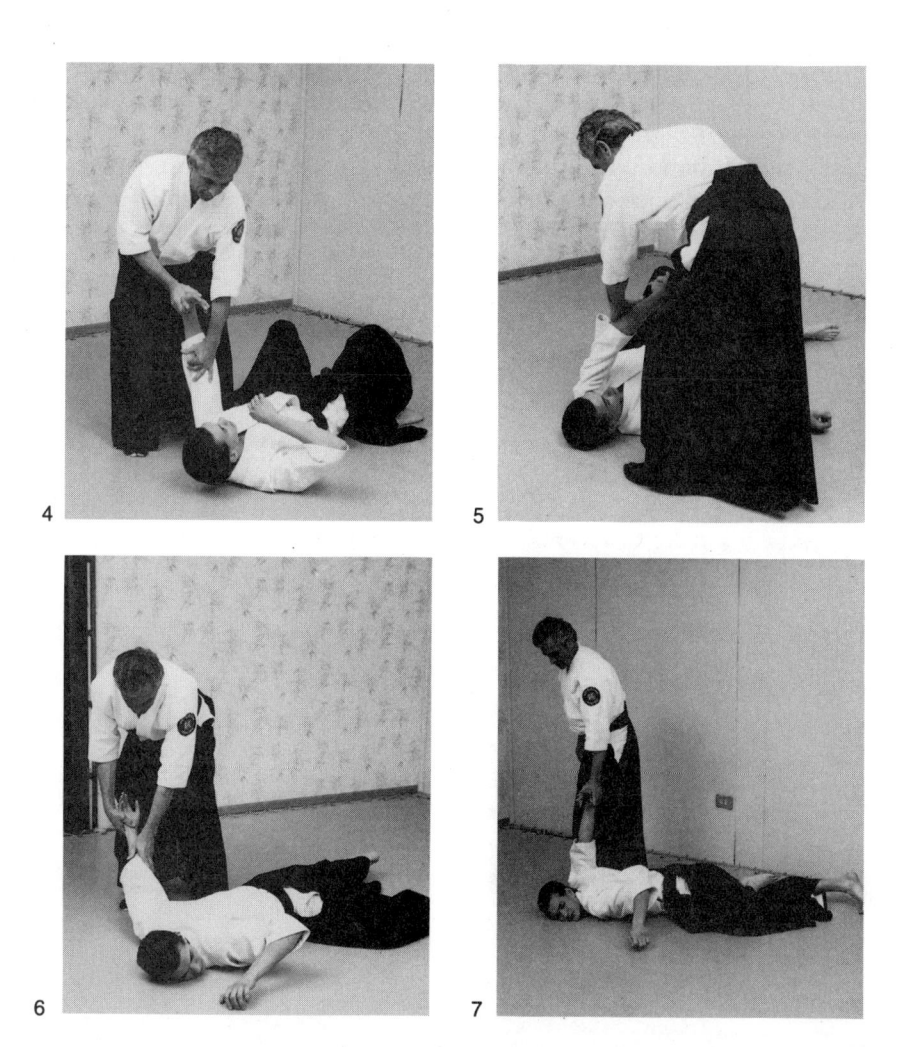

4

5

6

7

TECHNIQUE NO. 6

From behind, the opponent grabs the defender's gun with his right hand. With his right hand, the defender grabs the opponent's hand and turns in a right circular motion, raising the opponent's arm up. With his left hand on his elbow, the defender continues the circular motion until the opponent is on the ground, where he applies a pin suitable for handcuffing.

1

2

Awareness and Maintaining Self-Control

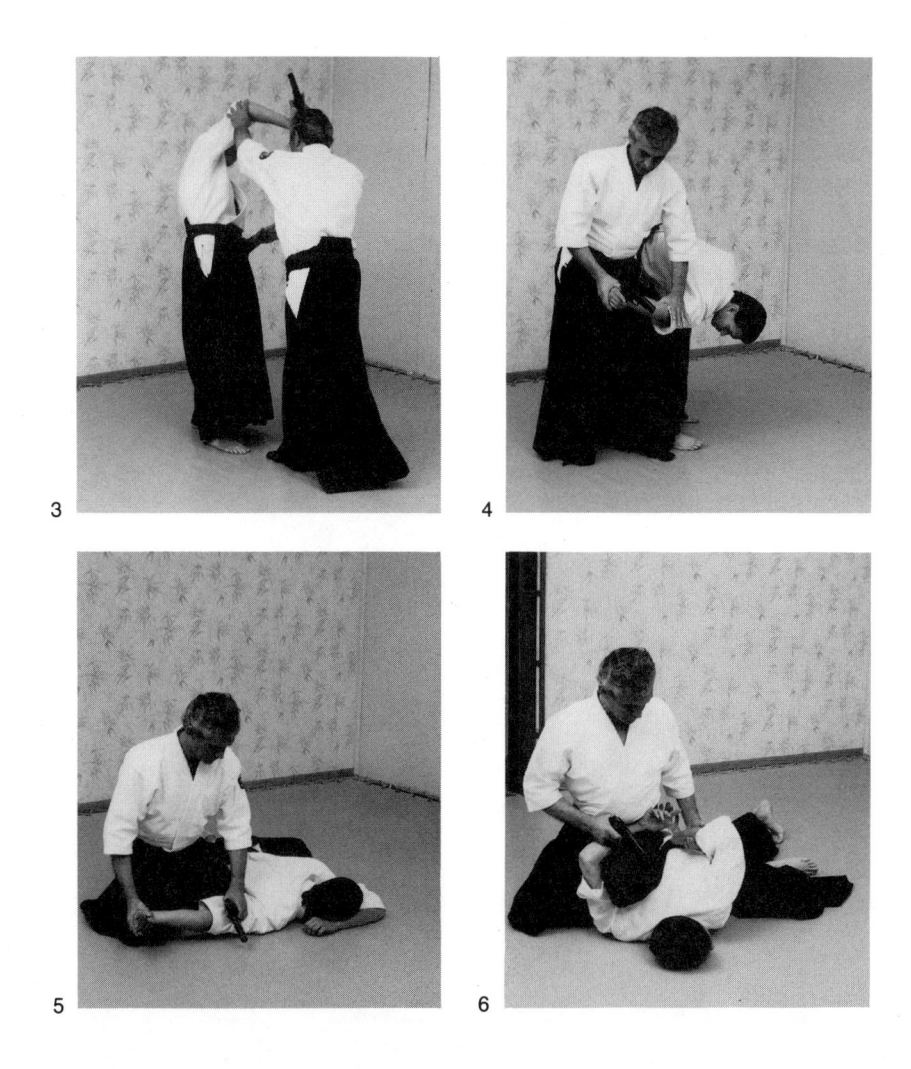

79

TECHNIQUE NO. 7

From the front, the opponent reaches for the weapon with his left hand. The defender places his left hand on the opponent's left hand, and with a circular motion raises it up, placing his right hand on the opponent's elbow. Then he leads him down to the ground into a leg pin suitable for handcuffing.

Awareness and Maintaining Self-Control

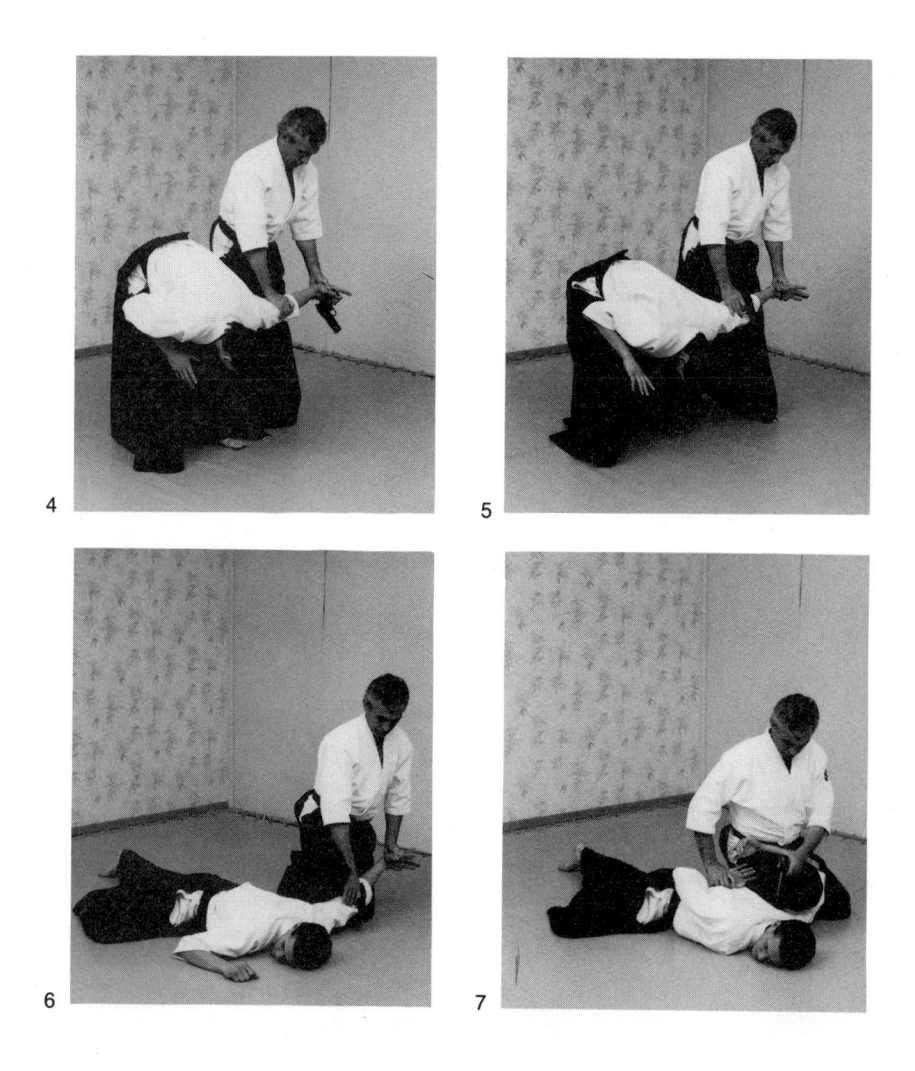

4

5

6

7

TECHNIQUE NO. 8

From the front, the opponent grabs the defender's right wrist with his right hand. The defender moves to the opponent's side, and with his left hand goes over and under the opponent's right arm, placing a forearm lock and throwing the opponent to the ground.

1

2

Awareness and Maintaining Self-Control

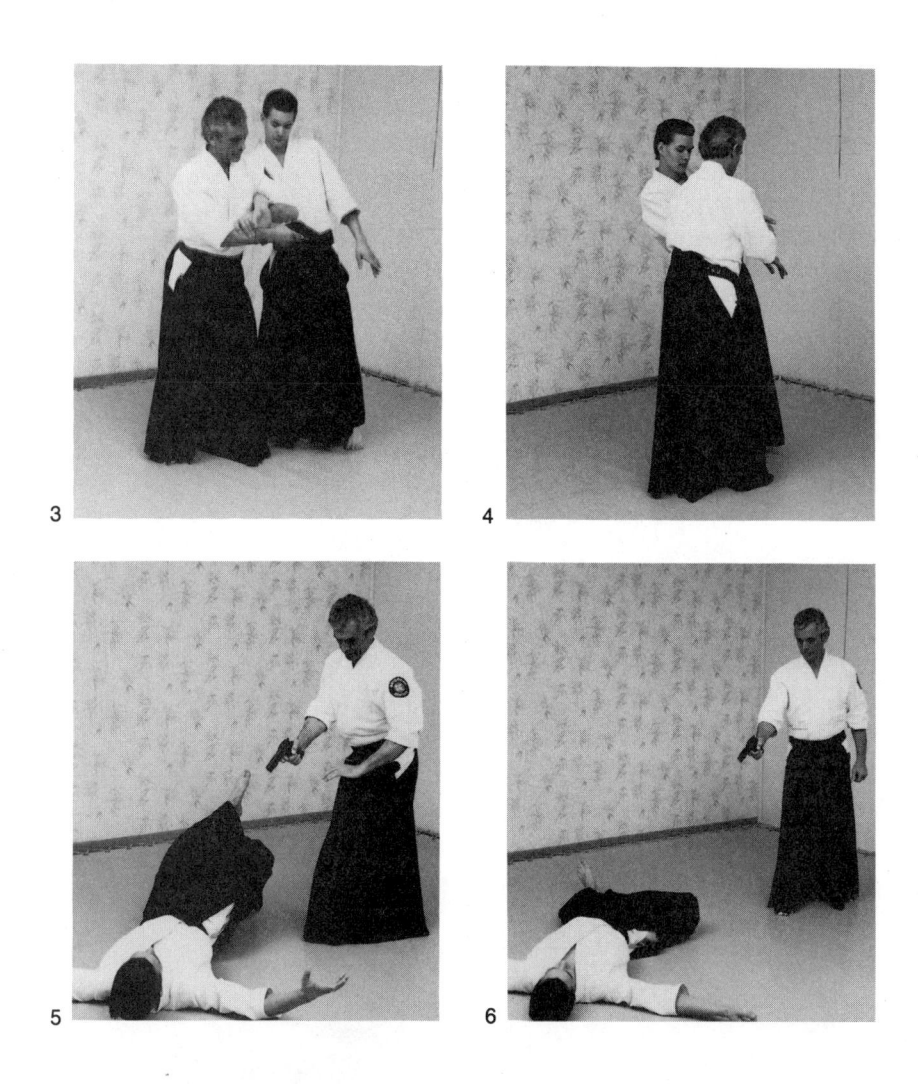

3

4

5

6

TECHNIQUE NO. 9

From the front, the opponent grabs the defender's right wrist with both hands. As the defender pulls his gun, he extends his right arm downward, places his left hand around the opponent's neck, and moving in right semicircular motion in front of the opponent, takes him down.

1

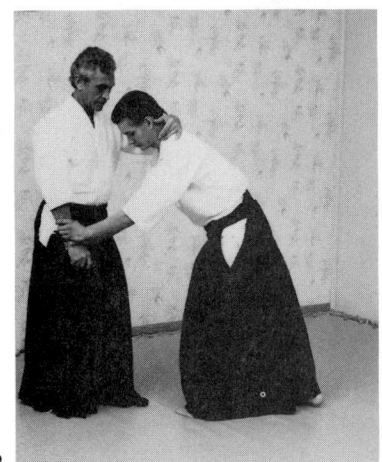

2

3

Awareness and Maintaining Self-Control

4

5

TECHNIQUE NO. 10

From the front, the opponent grabs the defender's right wrist with both hands. The defender sidesteps to the left, and with his left hand traps the opponent's left hand, bringing the gun over the opponent's left wrist. He applies downward pressure to bring him down into a leg pin, suitable for handcuffing.

Awareness and Maintaining Self-Control

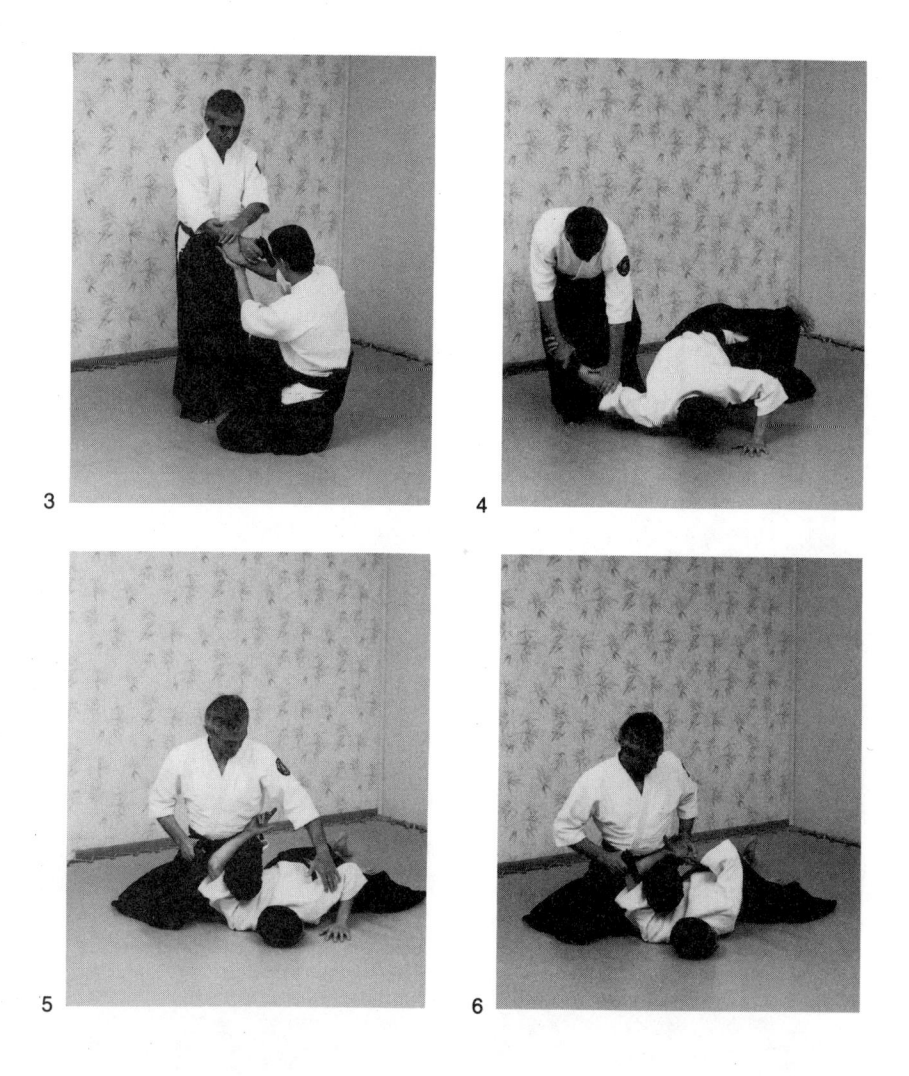

3

4

5

6

The Secrets of Police Aikido

TECHNIQUE NO. 11

From the front, the opponent grabs the defender's right wrist with his right hand. The defender traps the opponent's right hand with his left hand and moves his body under the opponent's right arm. He turns to the left and now has the opponent in a controlling technique called Sankyo (a wristlock). The next move is straight down followed by a pin, removing the weapon.

Awareness and Maintaining Self-Control

TECHNIQUE NO. 12

The defender sidesteps and parries the opponent's right punch to the face, with his left hand behind the opponent's elbow. He then steps forward, bringing his right arm across the opponent's neck and follows through with a choke takedown.

TECHNIQUE NO. 13

While the defender tries to draw his gun, the opponent grabs his wrist and simultaneously throws a hook punch to the face. The defender extends both arms and steps forward, leading the opponent down on his back. He then turns the opponent on his stomach and follows with a controlling pin.

1

2

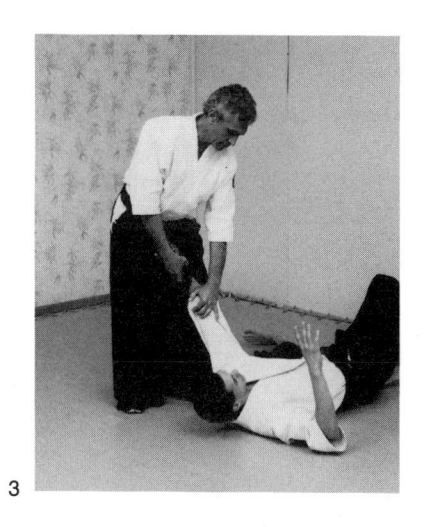

Awareness and Maintaining Self-Control

3

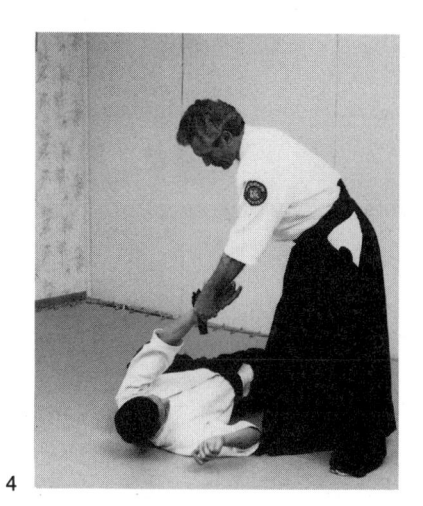

4

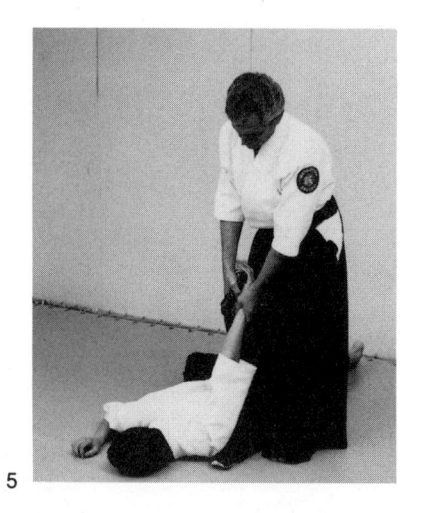

5

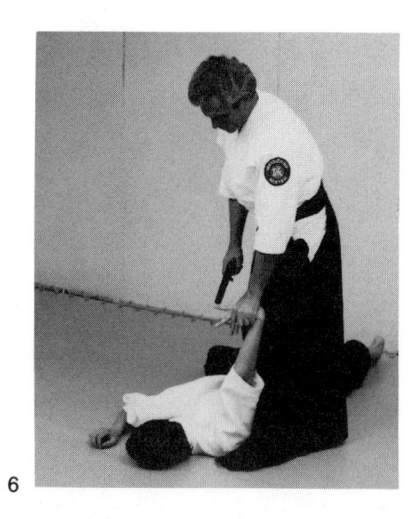

6

TECHNIQUE NO. 14

The opponent throws a straight left hand punch to the face. The defender sidesteps as he parries the opponent's elbow with his right hand. As the defender steps through, he brings his left arm over the opponent's elbow, breaking his balance and throwing him down on his back. He then turns the opponent over on his stomach and follows with a controlling pin.

Awareness and Maintaining Self-Control   93

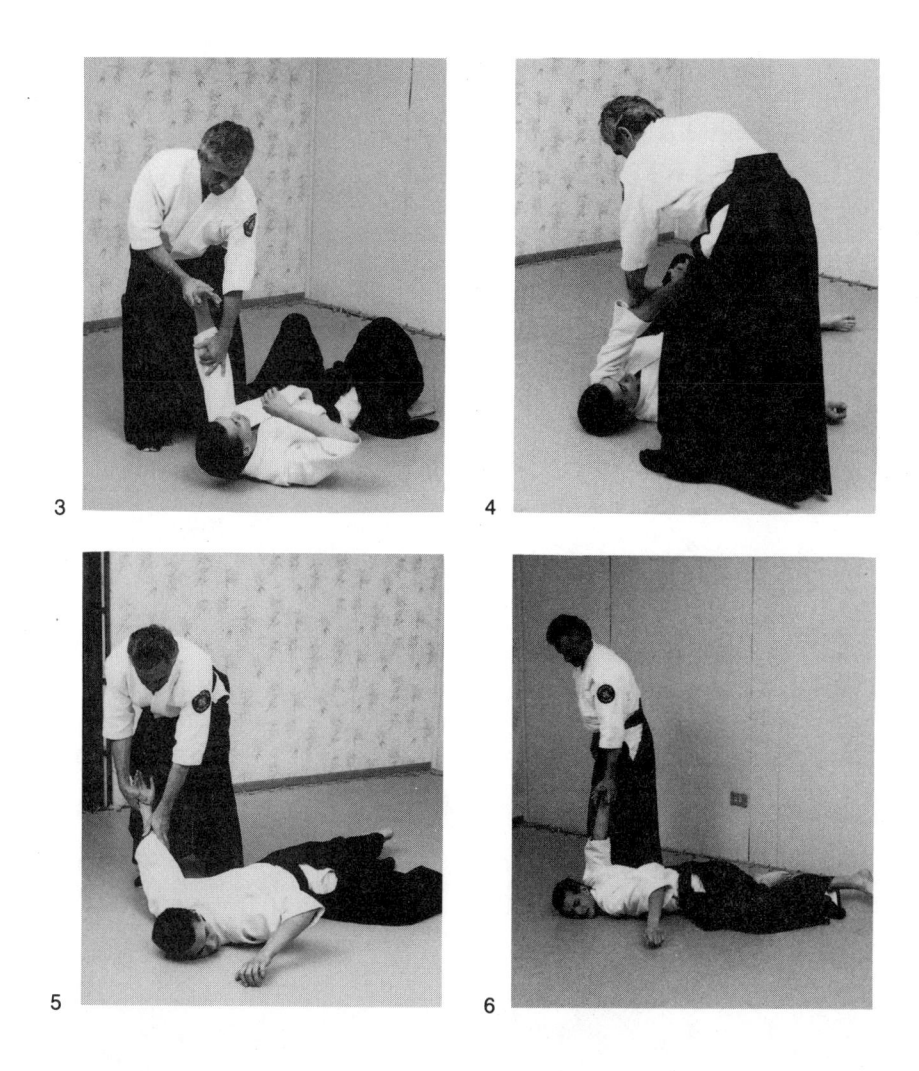

3

4

5

6

TECHNIQUE NO. 15

The defender sidesteps and parries the opponent's left punch to the face with his right hand. He then checks and brings the opponent's left arm down with his left hand. With his right arm, the defender chokes the opponent from the front and brings him down into an armlock and choke.

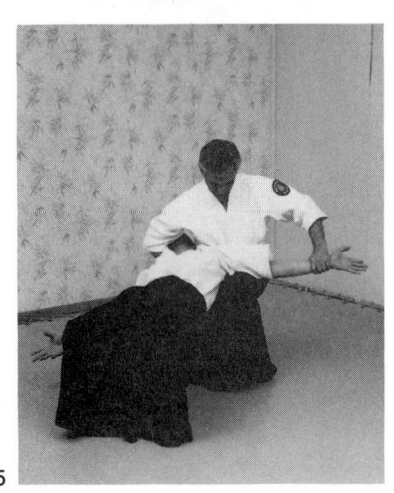

Awareness and Maintaining Self-Control

TECHNIQUE NO. 16

The defender sidesteps and parries the opponent's left punch to the face with his right hand. He then checks and brings the opponent's left arm down with his left hand. The defender moves behind the opponent, and with his right hand chokes and brings him down, at the same time extending the opponent's left arm over the defender's left leg.

TECHNIQUE NO. 17

The defender is bearhugged from behind. The defender extends his arms as he steps back, and is now in a position to control the opponent by taking him down by the elbow into a handcuff position pin.

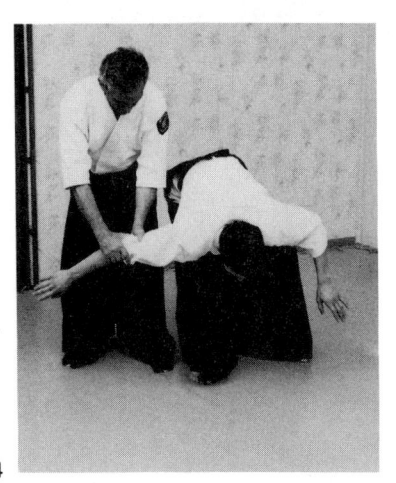

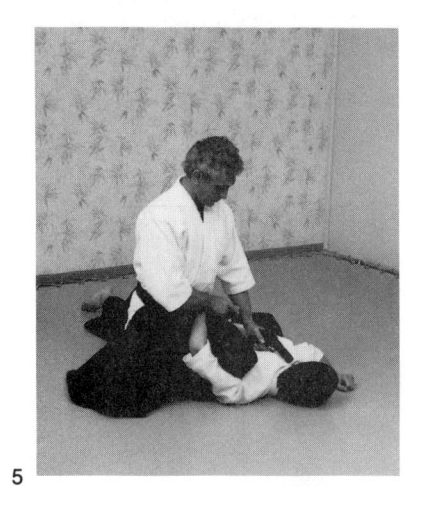

Awareness and Maintaining Self-Control

TECHNIQUE NO. 18

The opponent chokes the defender from behind. The defender grabs the opponent's elbow and drops down on one knee as the opponent falls forward on his back.

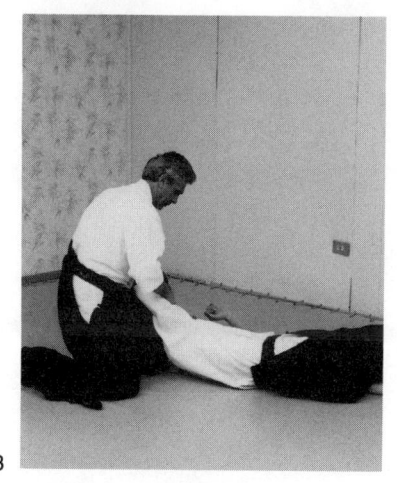

TECHNIQUE NO. 19

The opponent tries to hook punch the defender's face. The defender intercepts the punch with his left hand and at the same time punches with his right hand to the opponent's solar plexus. He then turns, and with his right hand grabs the back of the opponent's neck and drops to one knee, throwing the opponent on his back.

Awareness and Maintaining Self-Control 99

TECHNIQUE NO. 20

The opponent is on top of the defender, grabbing with the right hand and punching with the left. The defender intercepts the punch by extending his right arm on the inside of the punch and placing his left hand behind the opponent's right elbow. With knees bent, the defender simultaneously bridges his body and turns to the right, throwing the opponent off.

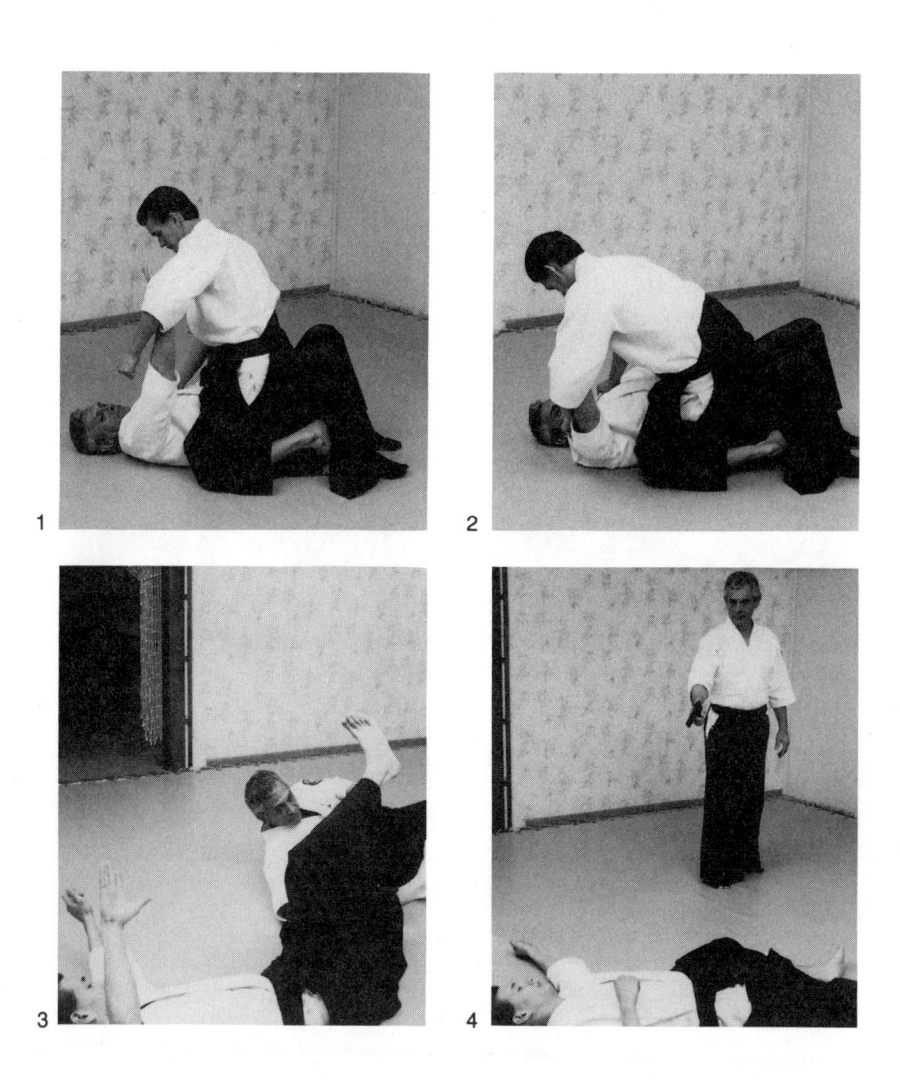

TECHNIQUE NO. 21

The opponent sits on the defender and chokes him with both hands. The defender bends his knees and places his hands on the opponent's elbows as he simultaneously bridges his body, turns to the right, and throws the opponent off.

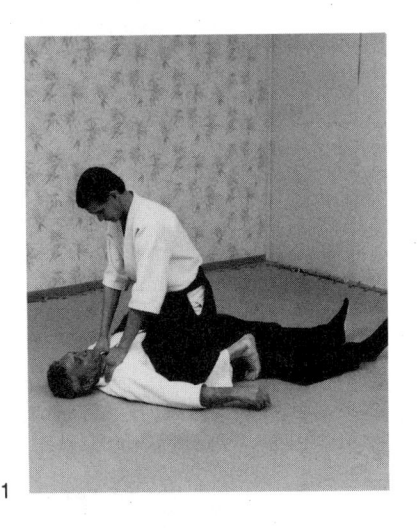

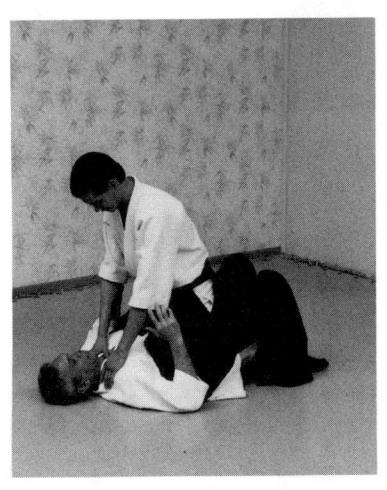

Awareness and Maintaining Self-Control

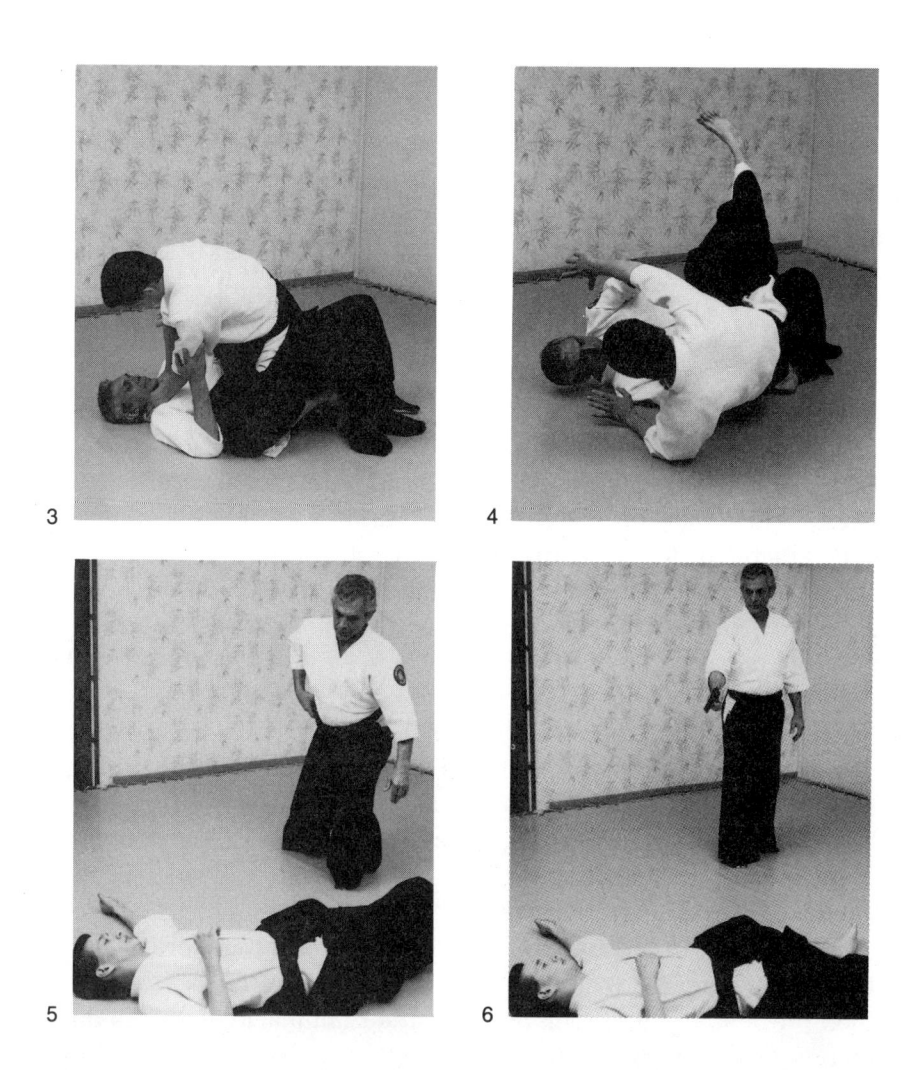

9 Police Officers' Testimony

The applications presented in previous chapters are based on traditional techniques commonly used in many dojos around the world. They were presented here not as they are typically, as a supplement to dojo training, but rather to provide a relatively simple and meaningful way to deal with unexpected attack. Very often, casual observers of Aikido presentations doubt the usefulness of the traditional techniques against real attacks. Anyone who has had these techniques demonstrated on him, however, has no choice but to become a firm believer. All of us are to some degree skeptical of new and unorthodox methods. Why should it be any different in the case of Aikido? I thought it would be of benefit to quote here from the personal experiences of real people. There can be no more convincing testimony to the effectiveness of Aikido in conflict than that of someone who has knowledge of the art and has been exposed to real conflict. I have therefore asked two of my students who are active police officers to write about their on-the-job experiences and how their familiarity with Aikido techniques and principles helped them to cope with these situations.

ROLE OF AIKIDO IN EVERYDAY LAW ENFORCEMENT

As a police officer in north central Texas with six years of experience, I know I haven't seen it all. Every day, I am surprised to encounter some new situation—and while I enjoy the challenge, I also know that I am expected to perform at a high level regardless of the circumstances. Recently I have found a tool that fits the constantly changing needs of police officers. This tool is Aikido.

Founded in Japan and evolved from a rich tradition of martial arts, Aikido could be defined as "the way to blend with universal energy." The Aikido student does not attack and destroy; rather he learns to live in harmony with his opponent while maintaining his own well-being. Any pain inflicted is momentary, and the techniques should never seek to cause permanent damage. Perhaps Aikido's greatest characteristic is that it takes this philosophy beyond mere physical techniques. Since undertaking the study of Aikido, I have had fewer fights on duty because I have learned not to clash with people *before* it becomes necessary to escalate to physical techniques. We spend a great deal of time talking about "blending" with the energy of others and then applying that idea to a technique. Aikido does not teach tactics for war; the Aikido student learns to be a lover of peace. Peace becomes a means rather than an end.

For example, another officer on my shift had arrested an intoxicated subject and was booking her into our jail. After finishing the book-in process he attempted to move her into the drunk tank. He was tired, agitated, and angry, as was the woman. When she saw the tank, she decided she wasn't going to go in. The officer decided that he had had enough of this and tried to physically push her in the tank, but she managed to prop her hands and feet against the frame of the door. She was a very large person, and the officer was struggling and pushing against her back and hips to no avail. She was in such a well-braced position she was able to overcome the officer's direct force. I calmly reached around the inside of her right elbow and, taking her right wrist, applied a wristlock. Not only had she lost one brace, but I was able to easily control her balance and move her into the tank without striking or injuring her.

Aikido is not limited to passively resisting suspects. One night I was dispatched to another intoxicated-person call, and found the violator sleeping in the courtyard of an apartment complex. I woke him up, and he said he lived just around the corner. We walked in circles for a minute, and it became obvious that he didn't know where he was going. He finally confessed that he lived several counties away and had no one to take care of him. I was left with no choice but to arrest him for public intoxication. He said that he would rather not go, and, in fact, he had just gotten out of the county jail and was involved in a suit over the conditions of the jail. I got him spread-eagled on a car in the parking lot and stood behind him when he started saying, "No, no." He turned to his left and tried to catch me with the back of his hand. I merely stepped back with his punch and caught his hand in front of me. I allowed his momentum to carry his hand past me, and then with a little wrist twist (*Kotegaeshi*) took him to the ground. I learned later that he had been in the county jail for breaking an officer's hand during another fight.

Finally, because we place a high importance on self-protection, we spend a significant amount of time on tumbling and learning how to fall. Recently this was very useful when I was the backup for a man on a gun call. The suspect was driving around the neighborhood and was supposed to be armed. I found him and followed him until the primary unit arrived, and we performed a standard felony traffic stop. The suspect raised his right hand and put a .25 caliber pistol to his head. We set up a perimeter and repeatedly attempted to establish communications, but before we were able to complete the perimeter the suspect went mobile. He passed by his own residence a block away and began to return to the site where he had been originally stopped. Before he got there, another officer used his squad car to partially block the street, and we surrounded him again. He switched the pistol to his left hand and again started to move. I ran up alongside the driver's door, grabbed his hand, and pulled the pistol away from his head. He discharged a shot straight up and accelerated the vehicle. I was still holding on to his hand but was unable to strip away the pistol. The truck's acceleration pulled me forward, and I would have otherwise hit the pavement very hard, but since learning to fall properly in my Aikido training, I was uninjured. (It turned out that the shot he fired was his last bullet. He drove another block, threw the gun out, and surrendered. Cops always want to know the ending.)

Aikido will take some time to understand and utilize. In fact, Aikido may best be understood as a process of self-perfection that may never be fully realized in this life. Nonetheless, I have found it to be a useful tool in dealing with stress, abusive persons, and self-defense.

Sgt. Michael A. Beutner No. 9
Denton Police Department
Denton, Texas

MENTAL AND PHYSICAL CONDITIONING TO SURVIVE

My past twenty years have been spent as a police officer for the city of Arlington, Texas. In reflecting back, I recall that after five years with the department, at the age of thirty-five, I started to become aware of my physical condition, or rather the lack of it. I was overweight, smoked and drank heavily, and did not exercise. The fact that I was overweight made me tired, and smoking left me short of breath. It is difficult to recall the numerous times I would awaken still hungover from late-night drinking, which left me with no energy to exercise. Sound like a vicious cycle? Absolutely!

Once I realized where I was headed, I began reading about various workouts and conditioning programs. I did not stop with reading about them, like most of my coworkers. I bought some weights, got together with my coworkers, and started to change my life. I also changed my eating habits. For many, that in itself could be the key to a better, healthier lifestyle. I went from a 40-inch to a 34-inch waist in the course of one year. Bearing in mind how long it takes to get out of condition, we shouldn't expect overnight miracles in exchange for years of abuse.

Mr. Sosa asked me to recall a life-threatening incident that happened to me within the past twenty years of law enforcement in which physical conditioning played a major part in my surviving it. I thought back, and even though I have been involved in many violent confrontations, I have never been hospitalized. Along with exercising, I developed a survival mind-set. Just being in good physical condition is not enough; you must also be in good mental condition. For just a moment think about what you have read. "The mind leads the body," but without a body to lead the outcome is guessed at, and so it is in reverse. Without a mind to lead, what can be expected of the body? In Aikido we are taught that the mind leads the body, and that means mental stability as well as being aware of our emotions, especially in confrontational situations.

Years ago I read that the definition of a survival mind-set is "the conscious or subconscious state of mind which maximizes a person's chances of surviving a critical incident." Roger Soloman Ph.D., a Washington state trooper, defined a critical incident in this way: "Any situation where one feels overwhelmed by a sense of vulnerability and/or lack of control over the situation."

We do not like to admit to others or ourselves when we feel this way. The simple truth of the matter is that each and every one of us feels different about an incident. Here are some common stages of a critical incident:

1. *Perception* A situation begins to unfold. We become altered by the perception of danger. Our perception is with our senses.
2. *Evaluation* We begin to analyze or evaluate the danger in two distinct phases:
    (a) If we focus on the danger, we tend to feel weak, helpless, and out of control. We could just "freeze."
    (b) If we focus on our abilities and capabilities of overcoming the danger, the feelings of weakness, helplessness, and lack of control decrease, while our feelings of strength and control increase. It enables us to cope with danger or fear more effectively, and allows us to move to the next phase.
3. *Formulation* Begin to develop a game plan. What is it that we have to do to establish control of the situation? What do we have to do to survive? Some people describe this as a feeling of resolve—they realize what has to be done and start doing it.
4. *Initiation* React. Respond. Do something.

It should be clearly stated that these four stages are often gone through subconsciously in a split second, and that a common factor in all critical incidents is fear. Fear is not panic. Fear is the emotion of alarm caused by the expectation or realization of danger. Every police officer has to learn to cope with fear or vulnerability.

Many think of the mind and body as separate entities, when in reality your mind and body are constantly interacting and working together. What your mind does will directly influence what your body does, and vice versa. It is this coordination of mind and body that makes it possible for one to control stress, improve the decision-making process, and enhance physical performance through mental conditioning. In the study of Aikido it is a key principle that is taught through techniques and exercises.

Although I have not given the reader a particular incident in police work that was critical to me, it is my hope that I have supplied a certain insight. Each of us will perceive a critical incident from an individual perspective.

Having considered the mind-set of survival, one must also give attention to physical conditioning. Without proper muscle development, it is almost impossible to coordinate the moves that must be made in the art of Aikido. Without proper muscle development around the joints, one will more than likely sustain injury, and injury due to ineffective muscle development will happen even on the mat at the dojo. Of greater consequence is the injury you may sustain while out in the field if you do not protect yourself against the attack of an opponent.

Being mentally and physically fit carries with it an extra bonus: commanding presence. I know you have heard this time and time again, but when you look and feel fit people take notice. They sense your own positive awareness. This is not a false confidence, but self-assurance that you are able to meet a given incident. You are not able to attain this when you are overweight, walking bent over, or breathing hard while climbing a flight of stairs.

People who stay fit have a "glow" of health. They tend to be less sick and recover from illness or injury quicker. Relate this to professional athletes. When injured, depending on the type of injury, they are back in a short time, and often show no signs of ever being injured. Think about the new trends for patients after major surgery. They are often urged to resume physical activity in order to recover at a faster pace and shorten their hospital stay.

Being physically fit adds more productive years to your life. Studies have shown that on the average, a police officer's life expectancy is only two and a half years after he retires. The lack of conditioning catches up to us at an alarming rate and shows no mercy when it strikes.

The bottom line is that being in shape can reduce the risk of injury in any all-out confrontation or workout. It gives us a sense of well-being that translates into self-confidence, and most important, adds healthy years to our lives.

> Rudi Panke
> Arlington Police Department
> Arlington, Texas

CONCLUSION

It is so important to remember the basic four principles of coordinating mind and body that I will again list them as a reminder:

1. Keep one point.
2. Relax completely.
3. Keep weight underside.
4. Extend Ki.

The physical and the mental aspects of Aikido are embodied within these four simple principles. During our training we must strive to maintain these points well, whether we are throwing someone or are being thrown. Once all Aikido principles are totally internalized, the resulting state of mind allows us to see through even the most complex situations.

Remember, too, the importance of a well-maintained body in any martial arts training. It is difficult to imagine the possibility of responding to physical threats without being physically fit.

Finally, I would like to stress, once again, the importance of the idea known as Shodo-o-Seisu. Once a student reaches an appropriate state of mind, backed by a strong and healthy body, the techniques will begin to flow smoothly and naturally. To reach this state it is necessary to penetrate the meaning of Ki, one point, and readiness. Through our training we must develop the ability to find the manifestation of these ideas during activities in the dojo and eventually in our daily lives. The only way to cultivate that type of clarity of mind is by devoting ourselves, in the words of Musashi Miyamoto, "to the assiduous study of the Way."

BASIC AIKIDO TERMS

Ai   harmony, blending, oneness
Ai hanmi   uke and nage using the same foot stance
Aiki   blending with universal energy, or oneness with Ki
Aiki-taiso   a series of calisthenics for the more often used Aikido movements derived from actual Aikido techniques
Atemi   pertaining to strikes
Bokken   wooden sword
Budo   way of life through application of martial arts principles
Bushido   the way of the warrior or his code of conduct
Chi   the Chinese equivalent of Japanese Ki
Chudan   middle position
Dan   black-belt rank
Do   path, road, or way of life
Dojo   a place of learning or training hall
Doshu   title of the present leader of Aikido
Funakogi undo   a rowing exercise developed to create motion and unbalance an attacker
Fudoshin   the undisturbed mind
Gi   training uniform
Hakama   baggy trouser-like garment worn by Aikido students and traditionally worn by the samurai
Hanmi   a natural ready stance with either right or left foot foward forming a triangle
Hanmi Handachi   uke attacks from a standing position while nage defends from a kneeling position
Hantai   opposite side
Happo undo   eight-direction exercise that trains the mind and the body to cover a 360-degree circle
Hara   abdomen
Hidari   left

Hiji elbow
Hiji-otoshi elbow drop
Ikkyo number one controlling art in Aikido
Irimi to enter in a straight line
Isshin one mind, or single-mindedness
Jiyuwaza medium speed freestyle against specified attacks
Jo wooden staff used for forms practice
Jodan high position
Joriki power of concentration
Jujinage crossed arm throw
Jogi kata forms practiced with jo staff
Kaiten-nage windmill throw
Kamiza a small shrine located at the front of the dojo
Katsujin-ken the sword to let live
Kata tori lapel grab
Katate tori wrist grab
Katate tori tenkan turning and blending with an opponent's wrist grab
Katate tori ryote mochi two hands grabbing one wrist
Kengi sword (bokken) form
Kesa-gake diagonal cut from the shoulder to hip
Ki the vital force of the Universe and the source of all energy. Every living thing is made of Ki.
Kiai a loud shout to focus energy
Kubishime choke
Kohotento undo a rocking exercise used as a principle for backward rolls
Kokyu breath
Kokyudosa an exercise that helps develop powerful energy flow (Ki) from a strong and balanced center
Kotegaeshi a technique applying pressure to the wrist to bring an opponent down
Kotegaeshi undo warmup hand exercise, wrist turnout
Kokyunage timing throw in Aikido
Koshi hips
Koshinage throw using the hips
Kyu ranks under black-belt level
Ma-ai proper distance between defender and attacker
Migi right side
Munetsuki straight punch to the abdomen or chest
Nage defender, or person who executes the technique

Basic Aikido Terms

Nikkyo undo   exercise to stretch the wrist and arm
O-Sensei   great teacher, referring to the founder of Aikido, Morihei Ueshiba
Sensei   teacher, one born before
Randori   freestyle against multiple attack
Ryokata tori   grabbing the shoulders with both hands
Ryote tori   holding both wrists
Samurai   term referring to Japanese warriors
Sankyo undo   warm-up hand exercise, wrist twisting
Seiza   Japanese sitting position with legs crossed under
Sempai   a student senior to oneself
Shihan   master teacher
Shihonage   four-corner throw
Shikko   samurai walk, walking from the kneeling position
Shodo-o-Seisu   controlling the first move
Shomen   the front of the dojo
Shomenuchi   strike to the top of the head
Sono mama   things as they really are, or suchness
Suwari-waza   techniques done from the sitting position
Tachi-tori   disarming sword (bokken) attacks
Taiken   body knowledge
Tanto   wooden knife
Tekubi   wrist
Tekubi shindo   wrist-shaking exercise to calm yourself
Tenchinage   heaven and earth throw, with one hand pointing upward and one downward
Tenkan   to turn, rotating around a vertical axis
Tori   to grab
Ude   arm
Uke   your partner in training taking the falls
Ukemi   the art of falling and establishing a harmonious relationship with the ground to eliminate injuries
Undo   exercise
Ushiro   from behind
Ushiro kata tori   grabbing both shoulders from behind
Ushiro kubishime   choke from behind
Ushiro tekubi tori   grabbing both wrists from behind
Ushiro hiji tori   grabbing both elbows from behind
Waza   techniques
Yoko   side
Yokomenuchi   strike to the side of the head

Basic Aikido Terms

Yonkyo a pressure point method of gripping and controlling an opponent's arm
Yudansha pertaining to black-belt rank holders
Zanshin awareness, extension of the mind, and follow through
Zenpo forward direction

REFERENCES

Miyamoto, Musashi. *A Book of Five Rings* translated by Victor Harris (The Overlook Press, 1974).

Saotome, Mitsugi. *The Principles of Aikido* (Shambhala Publications, 1989).

Sosa, Bill and Robbins, Bryan. *The Essence of Aikido* (Unique Publications, 1987).

Stevens, John. *Three Budo Masters* (Kodansha International, 1995).

Stevens, John and Shirata, Rinjiro. *Aikido: The Way of Harmony* (Shambhala Publications, Inc., 1984).

Takuan, Soho. *The Unfettered Mind: Writings of the Zen Master to the Sword Master* translated by William Scott Wilson (Kodansha International, 1987).

Tohei, Koichi. *What is Aikido?* (Rikugei Publishing House, 1962).

Ueshiba, Kisshomaru. *The Spirit of Aikido* translated by Taitetsu Unno (Kodansha International, 1984, 1987, 1990).

Ueshiba, Morihei. *The Art of Peace* translated by John Stevens (Shambhala Publications, 1992).

Yagyu, Munenori. *The Sword and the Mind* translated by Hiroaki Sato (The Overlook Press, 1986).

ABOUT THE AUTHOR

Bill Sosa is the founder and director of the International Aikido Association, with affiliated schools in the United States and Mexico. He has been practicing the art of Aikido for over thirty years.

Mr. Sosa has instructed the Dallas SWAT team and various other police departments. He has taught relaxation and centering principles as well as the proper use of energy to hospital staff and employees. In 1994 he was a guest speaker for the Doctors Sclerotherapy Convention in Tucson, Arizona, where he spoke on the health benefits derived from Aikido training. He introduced Aikido to Southern Methodist University and Mountain View Community College, where it is now an accredited course. He has also taught at other community colleges in the Dallas–Fort Worth area.

In 1987 he cowrote *The Essence of Aikido,* and in 1993 he wrote and self-published the *P.A.C.T. Manual* (Police Aikido Controlling Tactics). His articles on Aikido have appeared in many major martial arts magazines, and he has been featured on television and radio talk shows.

Mr. Sosa teaches numerous seminars in the United States and Mexico throughout the year, as well as regular classes in the Dallas–Fort Worth metroplex. He is currently working on a book based on his research in health, nutrition, life experiences, and personal philosophy.